SOCCER TRAINING MANUAL

GOALKEEPER

Edited by MICK D'ARCY

D0048621

Library of Congress Cataloging - in - Publication Data

D'Arcy, Mick (Edited by)
        Soccer Training Manual - GOALKEEPER

ISBN Number: 1-890946-45-1
Library of Congress Card Number: 00-105337
Copyright © June 2000

All rights reserved. Except for use in a review. The reproduction of utilization of this book in any form or by any electronic, mechanical, or other means, now known or here after invented, including xerography, photocopying, and recording, and in any information storage and retrieval system, is forbidden without written permission of the publisher.

Art Direction/Book Layout
Kimberly N. Bender

Cover design:
Melanie Thomas Communications Design, L.L.C.

Editing and Proofing
Mick D'Arcy
Bryan R. Beaver

Printed by
DATA REPRODUCTIONS
Auburn, Michigan

REEDSWAIN INC
612 Pughtown Road • Spring City
Pennsylvania 19475
1-800-331-5191
www.reedswain.com

SoccerPlus CAMPS
20 Beaver Road • Suite 102
Wethersfield CT 06109
(800) KEEPER - 1 • (860) 563-6263
email:info@goalkeeper.com

SOCCER TRAINING MANUAL
GOALKEEPER

Edited by MICK D'ARCY

PUBLISHED BY
REEDSWAIN INC

Table of Contents

A NOTE FROM TONY DICICCO

This book is a unique offering. It is a collection of articles that have been written by myself and the SoccerPlus Directors over the years and inspired by you, our students and my experiences with US National Team goalkeepers. Within this book you will find help for all aspects of your game; Physical, Technical, Tactical and Psychological.

As with all you receive from SoccerPlus this book is a tool. If you use it properly you will learn, develop and become a more effective goalkeeper and soccer player.

I suggest that you read through this book **carefully**. Do not try and read it all at once. Select different topics which you would like to learn more about and concentrate on those areas. Remember to do the written and mental exercises as well as the physical exercises. Open your mind to new ideas and see yourself evolve as a soccer player and person. As owner and founder of SoccerPlus Goalkeeper School, your evolution is my ultimate goal.

As your personal coaches, we encourage you to continue your pursuit of excellence in goalkeeping. For those of you who have attended our camp you know that the training continues long after the last session at camp. We thank you for the opportunity to train together and look forward to seeing your progress in the future.

Good Luck,

Tony DiCicco
President & Founder

A NOTE FROM MICK D'ARCY

The SoccerPlus Student Training Manual has been designed to help you in your training throughout the year. As is our wish at camp we want to share our goalkeeper knowledge and experiences with you. Experience is a key component to goalkeeping. Hopefully by sharing our experiences, your development will progress quickly.

This Training Manual is a collection of articles that have been written by members of the SoccerPlus family. Some you may have read previously in our newsletter The Keeper's Line, others were written specifically for this publication. Special thanks to Tony DiCicco not only for his excellent goalkeeper articles but also for his insight into international goalkeeper training with The US National Team.

In addition to Tony DiCicco and Mick D'Arcy, several articles were written by Shawn Kelly, Michael Milazzo and other SoccerPlus Directors past and present. Paul Cacolice, ATC, CSCS is the fitness and conditioning expert for SoccerPlus. His articles will give you a clear insight into what it takes to get your body ready to play at the elite level.

A special word of thanks to Shawn Kelly for his input on the design and appearance of the manual and to Carolyn Cacolice for her help in typing and proof reading endless articles.

The opinions expressed are those of our writers I hope that these articles provoke thought into the goalkeeping. Whereas we never say there is a 100% perfect way to play in the goal I am confident that information presented here will undoubtedly help you become a better keeper.

Enjoy,

Mick D'Arcy
Editor
National Director, SoccerPlus Goalkeeper School

EVALUATION OF GOALKEEPERS

What are the qualities that collegiate coaches look for in high school goalkeepers? What traits do ODP regional staff wants to see in state goalkeepers? What makes one keeper better than another? These are questions that are often asked by aspiring young keepers at camp. There is no definitive answer since each coach has his own set of priorities but there are certain goalkeeping characteristics that are appreciated by all coaches. Consistency is probably the most important characteristic that coaches look for. There is a lot to be said for the goalkeeper who makes the saves that he should make. Here are some of the main goalkeeping qualities broken down into the four basic elements.

TECHNICAL

Catching and Parrying: Catching is a fundamental skill for goalkeepers. You should be able to catch the ball comfortably and not give up many rebounds. Keepers should also be able to recognize when to catch and when to parry.

Diving: Only dive when you have to. A good coach will recognize when a keeper is showboating. It is better to makes saves look easy rather than difficult. Again rebounds are frowned upon.

Breakaways: Is the keeper aggressive or passive on breakaways? Does the keeper steal ground effectively and stay composed? Is the keeper brave? How is his depth perception on reading through balls? Does he risk injury when diving at a forward's feet?

High Balls: The ability to control the box is crucial. The keeper should make a clear keeper call and catch the ball at its highest point. Good keepers are able to absorb fair contact in the air and still hold onto the ball.

Distribution: Even a novice coach will be able to critique your distribution. Every goalkeeper should be able to take his or her own goal kicks, punt, drop kick and throw the ball effectively. How effective is the keeper in dictating the tempo of the game? Does he look for quick outlet passes and is his distribution as effective when rushed? Short distribution should be supported especially when changing the point of attack.

Foot skills: This used to mean goal kicks and punting but know keepers must be able to use their feet to deal with back passes and help relieve pressure. Good foot skills means the keeper is comfortable playing long and short passes with both feet.

Stance: The keeper should generally be on his or her toes in anticipation of being called into action. A good stance is a sign that he is prepared.

TACTICAL

Angle play: This area alone separates the pretenders from the contenders. By simply taking up the right position you can make goalkeeping look very easy.

Communication: An ounce of prevention is worth a pound of cure. The goalkeeper who can organize the defense and prevent the opposition from making scoring opportunities is invaluable. Don't confuse communicating with cheerleading. Keeper talk should be short, clear and concise.

Anticipation: Otherwise known as reading the game. The keeper should have a soccer brain to understand what is happening on the field so he can help his team solve problems.

PHYSICAL

Strength and Power: At the higher levels goalkeepers need explosive power to get to balls outside of their comfort range. They must also be physically strong enough to absorb physical contact especially on cross balls. Coaches will often ask prospective players how high is their vertical leap.

Flexibility, Agility and Coordination: A common nickname given to good keepers is "Cat" in recognition of their flexibility, coordination and reaction speed. Good hand-eye coordination is essential.

Physique: There are no exact guidelines on what size a goalkeeper should be. Certainly history has shown us that great goalkeepers can come in all shapes and sizes. However, if you feel you are a little short or a little tall, try to over-compensate in other areas such as vertical leap or agility.

Appearance: Good goalkeepers tend to take a lot of pride in their appearance. Always wear the right equipment and look tidy in the goal. Looking good will not help you keep the ball out of the net but it will help you to make a positive first impression.

Fitness: The physical demands on a goalkeeper are a lot different than those for field players. However, you should still maintain a high level of fitness. If a coach comes to see you play and notices that you are out of breath in the warm ups he will not be impressed.

PSYCHOLOGICAL

Experience: The best programs and teams are looking for goalkeepers with experience; State Cups, Regionals, National Youth Team etc. They look for keepers who have already experienced success but who are still ambitious.

Leadership: Goalkeepers are often referred to as assistant coaches on the field. The position is unique in that you can see the whole field. A keeper who does not lead is not fulfilling his obligation to the team. These qualities should also be seen on the practice field leading by example.

Poise: The keeper must stay composed throughout the whole game. Coaches look for keepers who lead their team down the stretch. Poise can be demonstrated both verbally and physically. A keeper's body language can tell a lot, especially after conceding a goal. Good keepers do not self-destruct under pressure.

Attitude: Coaches want keepers who are able to sit, learn and wait for their chances. Very few freshmen start in college so it is important to have some patience and be a team player while you wait for your moment. Be prepared to take constructive criticism and realize that you still have a lot to learn.

Confidence: This is attained through achieving success. The keeper who has confidence in his play earns assurance and respect from the rest of the team and from opponents. However, the over confident goalkeeper can be destructive to the team. Be honest with yourself in respect to your ability. Be humble when celebrating your strengths but recognize and strive to improve your weaknesses.

Training Ethic: To achieve and maintain a high level of goalkeeping you must pay your dues on the practice field. Put yourself in a position where if the opportunity presents itself, you are prepared to be successful. Good training habits are contagious and as a leader you should set the example in training.

As you strive to achieve all of the qualities and characteristics above, try not to lose sight of the big picture. To succeed in college you must be successful on the field and in the classroom.

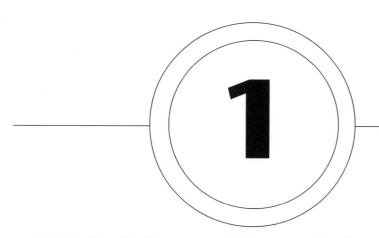

TECHNICAL

STANCE

The ready position or stance gets all of your body parts in place in preparation to make a save. A good stance allows you to move or react to a shot no matter where it goes. Combined with good positioning, your stance will help you make saves look easy.

The following list should help you evaluate your stance and act as a list of key reminders

1. Rest your weight on the balls of your feet. Your heels should be slightly elevated off the ground and your toes should point a little outwards.
2. Make sure your feet are even, with neither foot in front of the other. Your feet should be approximately shoulder width apart.
3. Bend your knees slightly so that you'll be ready to move in any direction.
4. To keep your body weight forward your waist should also be flexed. Check to make sure that your shoulders are in front of your feet.
5. Bend your arms and position your elbows equal to, or just in front of your chest.
6. Extend your hands with the palms raised. Your wrists should not be hyper extended. Your hands and fingers should be relaxed and positioned slightly above the height of your elbows.
7. Like the rest of your body keep your head and neck relaxed. Do not tilt your head. Move your body so that you are facing the play with your eyes focused on the ball.

Executing each of the seven points listed above is not difficult in a stationary mode. Almost every goalkeeper can perform the task upon request. It becomes much more difficult under live circumstances. Imagine you have just parried a shot. The ball rebounds out about 10 yards from you. A forward gets to the ball first. You get up on your feet and prepare for the shot. NOW do you have the right stance? In reality this is where it breaks down for most goalkeepers. Common errors include feet too far apart or leaning backwards. My point is that this is the true test of your stance. When you have been forced out of position, you recover and then you must get set for the shot. An easy way to train this is to have a player serve balls to you at the near post. Make that save and then shuffle across the goal to make a save from player #2 who is striking a ball at you from the penalty spot. The object here is not to make flying saves. Ask the servers to play balls at you. Upon saving the ball, freeze, take a look at your stance and make any corrections that you need to make.

CATCHING

Four Ways to Catch a Ball

The biggest difference between goalkeepers and field players is the rule that allows a goalkeeper to handle the ball. This simple statement clarifies why it is so important that a goalkeeper be able to catch the ball. There are basically four different ways to catch a ball; the basket catch, the contour or W catch, the side contour catch and the high contour catch.

Before we look at each of these catches there are some guidelines that should be applied to all catching techniques.

1. The hands must be relaxed and coordinated, allowing them to touch the ball at exactly the same time. If one hand gets to the ball first, chances of holding on are greatly diminished. Balls shot directly at the keeper are most easily caught because both hands are naturally lined up at about the same distance from the ball. Conversely, balls to one side or the other create a situation where one hand has to travel further to meet the ball than the other hand (more balls are dropped under this situation).

2. The arms should be relaxed and flexed at the elbows. There should be a cushioning or "giving" as the ball arrives. Do not over-exaggerate this absorbing of "giving" movement of the arms. If the arms are too active, it will cause you to arch your back and pull your head out of the catching area.

3. The head must be still and straight (not cocked to one side or the other). Bring the head, hands, eyes and ball together to complete the catch. Train the eyes in perception to disregard extraneous movement (like the swing of the leg as the ball is hit), but to see or perceive the ball only through the impact and subsequent flight.

4. Keep shoulders square to the catch. This means don't allow one shoulder to be closer to the ball than the other. Even when diving, both shoulders square themselves, thus creating a body barrier behind the hands. When the shoulders are square, the hands are naturally lined up to catch easily. The shoulders are square, the hands are well positioned and the body is creating a barrier.

Our philosophy is to simplify the references for catching. This allows the goalkeeper to evaluate and correct.

Now let's look at the four basic catching positions.

The Basket Catch - This position is used when balls are caught between chest height and the ground. The keeper creates a basket with the hands, forearms and upper body. Flexion is at the waist. It is very important to keep the forearms parallel, and to make sure that the body is squarely behind the ball.

If the body cannot be positioned behind the ball, don't use this catching technique (see side contour catching below). The implication here is that good keepers have good footwork, and good footwork allows goalkeepers to get into this position behind the shot. The nature of the basket catch allows two touches to control the ball. The ball is first touched and controlled with the forearm area; the second touch comes as the ball makes contact with the chest and is secured in the basket created by the hands, arms and upper body. If the ball comes to the chest first, the chance of a rebound off the body is much greater than if the shot is absorbed by the first touch of the forearm. We term this a "two-sound catch."

Contour Catch - We call it this because we want the hands to create the shape, or contour, of the ball. We want the wrist slightly flexed, not hyper extended. The arms should be extended, thus preparing the hands to receive the ball. The head should be still. The eyes should be focused on the ball. The contour catch is used for balls taken at chest height or above, whenever the goalkeeper can position the

body squarely behind the ball. Good footwork enables many top goalkeepers to catch using the contour position, rather than having to make a diving save (which is less secure, and more likely to cause a rebound). This catch is one-touch and one-sound. If both hands are not symmetrical and working together - actually making contact with the ball at the same time - the likelihood of retaining the catch is greatly reduced. For keepers that's bad news, because rebounds mean goals.

Side Contour - This position may become necessary if the body cannot be positioned squarely behind the ball. Like the contour catch, this is another one-touch and one-sound catch. You'll use the side contour catch for 95% of your diving saves, ranging from simple collapse dives to extension dives.

The challenge with this catch is to bring the far hand across the body, and get it to the ball at the same time as the near hand. If one hand arrives after the other, it will be difficult to hold the ball. We use the phrase "Bring the head, eyes and hands to the ball," thus assuring that the head is in a position to enhance the catch. The shoulders remain square to the field. The goalkeeper is on his side, not his chest or back. It takes a lot of training to learn to catch in this position, especially as the pace of the shots increases.

High Contour - This catch is used for balls above an opponents challenge, before any striker can attempt to score from a head ball. This technique is essentially the same as the contour catch, but in a different catching area: above the head. Use the leg closest to the challenge to protect the ball. By using knee flexion and arm swing to transfer momentum up to the catch, the keeper can jump higher and have more dynamic balance and strength to catch while going up for the ball. Upon catching the ball the keeper then needs to protect the ball. The ball should be taken down to the chest and protected by the hands and arms.

The ability to hold on to the ball is often the difference between a good goalkeeper and a great one. Nothing demoralizes a forward more than a goalkeeper making a save and holding on to the ball. It is one of the basic elements of goalkeeping and one of the first skills that coaches notice when evaluating a goalkeeper.

"

"It's not necessarily the amount of time you spend at practice that counts; it's what you put into the practice."

Eric Lindros, Philadelphia Flyers

"

THE DIVING SAVE

The diving save is the most exciting save to see. It's featured on goalkeeping highlight tapes and it brings the crowd to their feet. However, it is important to remember that a goalkeeper should only dive as a final measure. If possible it is better to use quick footwork to get your body behind the ball and save without diving. Here's why:

1. You risk dropping the ball every time you dive.
2. Risk of injury is increased.
3. From a standing position you can start a counter attack quickly.
4. The keeper looks more composed without diving and makes the opposition think that they will need a perfect shot to score.

However, there are times when a goalkeeper has to dive to make the save. Diving saves tend to fall into two categories 1) the collapse dive and 2) the extension dive.

The Collapse Dive

By definition a keeper's feet do not leave the ground and the body attacks the ball in a slightly forward momentum while collapsing to the ground.

The first step in a collapse dive is literally your first step. If the ball is played to your right then your right foot should step forward at approximately a 45% angle. Your hands should move forward and meet the ball in a side contour style. From this position you bring the ball to the ground. The ball should be the first thing to hit the ground. The landing is crucial because you must hold onto the ball. The ball should be pinned against the ground with one hand on top of the ball and one hand behind. The ground acts as a third hand securing the ball in place. If the ball is shot along the ground the same principles apply; first step, drive hands towards ball, one hand behind ball and one on top, save in front of you and then protect the ball.

Your finishing position on the ground should have the ball a comfortable distance in front of you i.e. your elbows should not be tucked under your chest. Once you have landed safely with the ball then you can tuck it in to protect it. It is also important to make sure that you do not end up lying on your stomach or on your back. Your chest should be facing into the field of play. Many young goalkeepers find themselves falling backwards on collapse dives. The first step forward is important but if you do not drive your hands forward then you will fall backwards.

Simply stated, your arms are attached to your body. If your arms go forward the rest of your body will follow.

Extension Diving
(a.k.a. flying)

This is the save that was invented for highlight films. The ball has been shot. It is out of your reach. The only way you can reach it is with some quick footwork and to propel your body explosively through the air. Unlike the collapse dive your feet are airborne when you catch the ball. However, to make the big save in the air your first moves on the ground must be right.

In similar style to a collapse dive you take a forward step with the foot closest to the ball; but now you place your weight on that leg as you bend it like a coiled spring. Using your arms and opposite leg you then drive your body to intercept the ball. The movement should be explosive to get your body off the ground. Upon catching the ball you must continue to drive through the ball and begin your descent. The ball must be the first thing to hit the ground to absorb the impact. The arms, midsection and legs will follow. And again, like the collapse dive, your body should be facing the field of play upon landing. Because of its exciting nature some keepers tend to overuse the extension dive. Do not use this save until it is absolutely necessary. Remember "Great goalkeepers make saves look easy."

Words of Caution

Training or practicing diving saves can be hard on the body especially if your technique is not good. Do not over train to the point where you are so tired that technique will suffer and the likelihood of an injury will increase. Watch where you train. Find the softest patch of grass and work out there. Many professional clubs have large sand boxes for this purpose.

"

Success is a journey not a destination. The doing is usually more important than the outcome. Not everyone can be Number One.

Arthur Ashe

"

THE FRONT SMOTHER

In the course of a game a striker gets off a shot from 25 yards, close to the ground, with a lot of pace and it's directly at the goalkeeper. How often do goalkeepers face shots like these? How do they react to them? This is certainly not the time for a power dive, or a nonchalant bend over to collect the ball. It is time to use the front smother technique.

When executing the front smother it is most important to get the body into the path of the ball. Very often I have seen keepers try what I call the "side smother." This is actually a collapse dive using the technique of the front smother. This "side smother" often ends in an unfavorable result for the keeper because he has not positioned his body directly into the path of the ball. If a ball is not hit directly at the keeper, but within 1-2 yards a front smother may still be appropriate provided the keeper can use footwork to get into the path of the ball. This save is even more common on wet days when the ball is slippery. By getting your whole body behind the ball you reduce the risk of the ball squirming past you.

It is important for the keeper to bend at the knees while staggering the legs, one in front and one behind. This will help him get low on the ball and will reduce the margin for error. I have seen a number of keepers keep their legs together, straight, and very stiff, leaving the keeper with a long way to bend to get to the ball. In addition, this leaves the keeper in a very unbalanced position. The bent knees and staggered legs leave the keeper in a good balanced position, low on the ball, and ready to attack the shot.

Of course, we must prepare our hands to collect the ball. The keeper should have his two pinky fingers close together with elbows in to execute what is simply a basket catch. Bring the ball tightly to the chest while still low on the ball, but with the feet still on the ground. Many keepers try to "flop" down on the ball. This is not only painful to the keeper, but also provides a loss of control of the body. This may lead to errors.

Finally, let the forward momentum that the keeper has created by attacking the ball take them easily to the ground on the forearms. Since he has already positioned himself low on the ball the fall or dive to the ground should be minimal. Some goalkeepers complain about how much the front smother hurts them. If he has positioned himself correctly and has total control of his body the front smother should not be painful.

The Front Smother technique provides a very safe and effective way to collect balls in your "control zone." The next time you have the opportunity to watch a high level game see if the keeper uses this technique and how well it works.

Things to Remember:

1. Get the body directly into the path of the ball.
2. Bend at the knees with the legs staggered.
3. Prepare hands with pinky fingers together and elbows in.
4. Bring the ball tightly to the chest in a basket catch.
5. Let the low body position on the ball and forward momentum take you to the ground under control.

Grobbelar on the importance of soccer:

How could a seventeen year old forget seeing his best friends killed? How can he forget killing a fellow human being? The simple answer is that he cannot. Even now, years later, I still have nightmares in which I hear again the screams and see those frightened faces, before waking up in a cold sweat. After having experienced border raids, drugs, delousing, having to eat beetles because you are out of rations, and tracking terrorists, football hardly seems to be a matter of life and death. Losing a semi final is not a tragedy and missing a match because of a groin strain is not the end of the world. If war teaches you anything it is an appreciation for being alive and I will never apologize for laughing at life and enjoying my football.
　　* Grobbelar spent two years in service in the Rhodesian Army in the mid 70's

BREAKAWAY SAVES

Making the Breakaway Save

The breakaway save is a critical part of every goalkeeper's arsenal. The save comes in many different varieties, from a forward breaking through for a one on one from the halfway line to a ball squirming free during a goal mouth scramble. A goalkeeper has three options:1) Win the ball before the shot is taken, 2) Make the save as the forward is shooting or 3) Make the save after the shot has been taken. A variety of circumstances will dictate which approach should be taken. But whatever the circumstances the basic rules still apply. The following are 10 points you need to remember.

1. Give a "keeper" call when winning a free ball.
2. Hands should be first to the ball unless you are outside the box.
3. When the attacker is cutting in to the goal from an angle, attack the open ball with your hands closest to the near post
4. Keep your head low behind your hands and arms for safety.
5. Your angle of approach to the ball should be low and hard.
6. Follow through the ball after making the save.
7. Your body shape should be similar to diving i.e. hands and arms out front, chest facing the field and legs bent and slightly apart.
8. If the opponent still has the ball under control make yourself as big as possible in the goal while maintaining a "set" stance.
9. Once the opponent takes a touch decide whether to attack the ball or steal more ground.
10. After you win the ball protect it and then get up quickly to start the counterattack.

Let's look at each one of these points and analyze them further.

Give a "keeper" call when winning a free ball
By calling out "keeper" you are telling everyone (including yourself) that you are going to win the ball. Psychologically it lifts your defenders because they now

know that you have taken control of the situation. It also lets all players in the vicinity know to get out of the way because you are coming through.

Hands should be first to the ball unless you are outside the box.
The safest way to attack the ball is with your hands. Obviously if you win the ball with your hands it is easy to control in contrast to winning the ball with your feet in a sliding tackle. You have little control with your feet as to where the ball will end up. Your hands and arms also offer you more physical protection and you are less likely to get injured. Of course if you are outside the box you will need to tackle or clear the ball with your feet. The exception to this rule is when you are saving the ball at the same time that the forward is shooting. This is called smothering the ball. Instead of using your hands use the inside of your forearms to absorb the force of the shot. Your hand will be slightly bent to coral the loose ball.

When the attacker is cutting in to the goal from an angle, attack the open ball with your hands closest to the near post.
One of the golden rules of goalkeeping is Never Get Beaten on your Near Post. This is your foremost responsibility. This is often referred to as taking the shortest path to the ball. Also consider the repercussion if the ball deflects off your hands. If they are facing the nearest goalpost then the likelihood is that the ball will go out of bounds. However, if your hands are pointing into the field of play that is where the ball will go. This could lead to an open goal scoring opportunity for a second attacker.

Keep your head low behind your hands and arms for safety.
When performed incorrectly the breakaway save can be dangerous to both the goalkeeper and attacker. It is imperative that you use proper technique to avoid the risk of head injury. Sometimes it is impossible for the forward to avoid contact. In these circumstances you will avoid injury if you keep your head low to the ground and behind your arms. If the forward does make contact with your arms he will most likely fall over the top of your body and your arms will absorb the contact with little discomfort.

Your angle of approach to the ball should be low and hard.
Following on the previous point you should keep your body low for safety reasons but also to prevent the ball from slipping under your body. The analogy often used in this circumstance is that your body should resemble a jet plane and not a helicopter i.e. A jet plane approaches the runway low, hard and fast whereas a helicopter descends slowly and from high above. If you attack the ball like a helicopter your timing must be perfect. There is no margin for error. However, if you attack like a jet you still have a good opportunity to save even if you get there late because the forward will not be able to slip the ball underneath you.

Follow through the ball after making the save.

It is important that your body has enough momentum to follow through after making contact with the ball. First of all momentum will take you out of danger i.e. you will not stop dead in front of the forward. Momentum will give you strength in case of a collision with the forward. Secondly, should the ball squirm free you will find it in front of you rather than behind you.

Your body shape should be similar to diving i.e. hands and arms out front, chest facing the field and legs bent and slightly apart.

In the heat of the action it can be difficult to analyze your body shape. But if you follow the right technique you will feel that you have your body under control and protected at the same time. The easiest time to check your shape is at practice. After you make a save take a moment to look at your final position and shape.

If the opponent still has the ball under control make yourself as big as possible in the goal while maintaining a "set" stance.

This is where most inexperienced goalkeepers will make a mistake by trying to force the striker's hand. As daunting as it is standing in the goal as the striker bears down remember that the pressure is on the forward to make the right decision and score. Do not help the striker by committing yourself to going down when they still have the ball under control. A lot of forwards will wait for the goalkeeper to make the first move and then capitalize. If a forward dribbles the ball around you then you probably overcommitted too early. By standing up you will delay the striker and hopefully your defense will recover quickly to help.

Once the opponent takes a touch decide whether to attack the ball or steal more ground.

When the forward is attacking your goal in a one on one breakaway situation you must recognize when the forward is capable of getting a shot off and when he is chasing the ball. This simple skill will allow you to make the all-important decision: Should I be "set" or can I come out a little further to narrow the angle. If the forward shoots as you are coming out (stealing ground) he will often score since you are off balance. You should take short steps as the striker gets closer to you and the goal. However, if you hold your ground and stay in the "set" position then you give the forward a lot of goal to shoot at. The third component to be considered in making the decision is at what stage can you win the ball. This is of course your first priority. If you cannot win the ball then you decide between stealing ground and getting set. This simple decision making process is more difficult to grasp than one might imagine. Repetition at practice will sharpen your skills.

After you win the ball protect it and then get up quickly to start the counterattack.

After you have done the hard work of winning the ball, secure it in your possession until the immediate danger passes. However, do not stay on the ground any longer than you have to. Once you have the ball it is your responsibility to start your team's next attack.

Games to improve your breakaway skills
1
- Four goalkeepers and one field player in a 12 yd x 12 yd square
- 2 v 2 + 1
- Team with the ball keeps possession with their feet for as long as possible. Opposing goalkeepers try to win the ball back. When they do they become field players with the plus player.
- Play for one minute only at a time

2
- Place two goals 36 yards apart (2 goal areas). One goalkeeper in each goal.
- Six players behind each goal to the goalkeeper's right hand side with balls.
- First player dribbles towards opposite goal and attempts to score. As soon as the shot is taken an opposing player can attack the first goal. The first attacker now must recover and defend his goal.
- First team to 10 goals wins.

3
- Place balls 35 yards from the center of the goal.
- Players have 5 seconds to advance the ball and score in MLS shoot-out fashion.

These three games will give you plenty of opportunities to practice the three different types of breakaway saves: winning the ball before the shot, smothering the shot and saving shots. Don't forget that the forward is heavily favored to score on most breakaways. Sometimes you will do everything right and still give up a goal. Sometimes you will do everything wrong and the forward will miss an open goal. Concentrate on doing the right things technically and tactically and you will pull off your share of game winning saves

Breakaway Training Tips
1. During practice, field players should be encouraged to avoid contact with the keeper.
2. On breakaway training days wear long pants to avoid excessive wear on your body.

POINT BLANK SAVES

First, let me say, that no keeper can repeatedly save shots from close range. If the defense allows penetration and shots from inside the penalty spot, goals will be scored. Also numerous studies have shown that most goals are scored from the immediate area in front of the goal to the penalty stripe and just slightly wider than the goal. This area described is, without question, point blank.

Having mentioned all of the above, saves on these close "point blank" shots are very often game winners. When two equal teams are playing, scoring chances do not come frequently for either team. The ability of a keeper to make this kind of save more often than his or her counterpart might determine which team will win. Besides saving a goal this save can change the direction of the game. It's demoralizing for a forward to miss from close range and a huge lift psychologically for the defending team.

There are five major considerations in making this save.

Body weight must be forward.
Very often a keeper's body weight falls backward when faced with a "point blank" shot. When this happens, almost all shots regardless of their speed will find their way into the net. The keeper cannot adjust to save when he or she is falling backward. Make sure that you lead with your hands and keep your shoulders forward.

Movement across the goal must be controlled.
A common scenario leading up to point blank shots is the attacking team reaching the defending team's goal line and then serving across the front of the goal. When the ball is brought that deep and that close to the goal, the keeper is very often forced to play the front post. As the ball is played across the front of the goal, the keeper must move quickly to cover the unprotected side of the goal. A common fault is moving across the goal too quickly and uncontrolled as almost every shot at or behind the keeper will go in and most shots to the far post still find the back of the net. In this situation, the keeper must center his body weight

just before the shot is taken. He will probably not be in perfect position, but he must be in control of his movement, otherwise adjusting to the location of the shot is almost impossible.

Step out and pressure the shooter.

It's no secret that goalkeepers have to be brave. Psychologically you need to have the right attitude to make this save. There can be no fear of being hit by the ball. Frankly the object is to get your body into a position where the striker will hit you with the ball. If a keeper tries to play a point blank shot close to the goal line, most deflections will still find the net. The keeper must take a step or two towards the striker. This accomplishes a couple of things: **a)** A shooter by instinct tries to shoot wide of the keeper, by stepping out just prior to the shot, the keeper, in effect, makes the goal smaller. Now the shot can either hit the keeper or go wide; **b)** By stepping out the keeper improves his angle of deflection. Balls that he deflects will have a better chance of rebounding wide of the post rather than just inside the post. **c)** The forward is more likely to be intimidated by an on rushing keeper than one who stays on the line. By forcing the striker to avoid contact with you, you may force him to change his shot. REMEMBER: Stepping out makes the goal smaller for the shooter, but the keeper's weight must still be forward.

Saving movements of the keeper are timed with the touch of the ball off the striker's foot.

Many keepers' take in too much movement prior to the ball actually being struck by the foot or head. The keepers have already anticipated the shot and have lost their saving shape by standing up and big (weight forward). Respond to the touch of the ball off the foot or head and react to that touch. Understand that not every ball will be saved, just as in a game, this is a very difficult saving situation. Don't be discouraged, just keep training and this big save will happen for you and your team.

Don't forget the second save.

It is rare that a goalkeeper is able to hold the ball on a point blank save. We are usually thrilled to "get in the way" of the first shot. As a result there will always be rebounds and second opportunities for the strikers. Of course you hope that your defenders will come to the rescue and clear any loose balls. But you still need to be prepared to recover and make a second save.

The odds are stacked in favor of the striker who gets a clean shot off in this range. The goalkeeper's job is to reduce the odds. Don't be frustrated by a lack of success in this area. Like penalties you are often at the mercy of the striker's competence and composure in point blank situations. But if you follow the five tips above you will find that you will increase your chances of pulling off "the miraculous save".

PARRYING THE BALL

The goalkeeper's first reaction to any shot should be to successfully catch the ball. If, however, the ball is hit out of the keeper's catchable range, or if the keeper feels he cannot hold onto the ball due to slick conditions, another option is to parry the ball. By parrying the ball the keeper redirects the flight of the ball to the outside of the goal. There are two types of parries: **1)** The fingertip parry, and **2)** The heel-of-the-hand parry.

The fingertip parry is a technique used when an uncatchable shot is hit soft enough that the keeper's fingertips are able to redirect the ball. Using the fingertips will give the keeper more accuracy when parrying the ball. The idea is to change the flight of the ball from going into the net, to sending the ball wide or over the goal. Although this will concede a corner kick, it will not allow a shot off the rebound with the keeper out of position. Many inexperienced keepers will drop an uncatchable ball for a rebound shot. Using the parry will prevent the ball from rebounding into danger. Again, it is better to give up a corner kick than to give the opposing team a three-yard shot at an empty net.

The heel-of-the-hand parry technique is used when the uncatchable shot is hit too hard for just the keeper's fingers to affect the flight of the ball. The heel is the part of the hand at the bottom of the palm and just above the wrist. Using the heel of the hand will allow the keeper to deflect a hard shot with force sending the ball far from danger.

The physical progression for parrying the ball is the same for the collapse dive and the extension dive. Remember to step forward, towards the ball with your near foot. Extend your near leg and drive the opposite knee. This will propel you towards the ball. Always try to catch the ball first; but if the ball is uncatchable for any reason, use the parry and get the ball out of danger.

Things to remember when using the parry:
- Use the fingertips on softer, uncatchable shots. Using the fingertips will give the keeper more accuracy.

- Use the heel of the hand on hard, uncatchable shots. Fingers may not be strong enough to redirect a hard shot.
- Low shots to the corner: try to parry the ball out wide, around the post, putting the ball over the end line.
- High shots to the corner: either parry wide or over the goal. Again, send the ball over the end line and out.
- Do not try to slap the ball, just change the direction in which the ball is heading.
- Do not stop the ball. Make the decision to catch or parry the ball away.

TRAINING METHODS TO IMPROVE PARRYING SKILLS

- Depending on the keeper's technical level and confidence, work on simple and functional stages.
- Try functional training where the keeper must decide to catch or parry. Make your keeper take shots low and high into the corner. Velocity will determine fingertip or heel, so change the speed of shots.
- Try this progression: start the keeper off at a post on his/her outside knee. Roll the ball to the opposite post, forcing the keeper to use correct footwork and parry the ball wide. Have the keeper reload and work to the other side. Next have the keeper start at a post in a stand-up, ready position. Send an uncatchable ball to the opposite post forcing the keeper to use the parry technique. If more than one keeper is training at a time, then once a keeper makes the save, force him/her to go back to the starting position by going between the server and the next keeper. This will create more confusion and allow the keepers to train in a game-like situation. Set up targets for accuracy.

Glenn Hoddle on Pat Jennings:
Pat was brilliant in many games but some of the things he did in training were little short of astonishing. In shooting practice he might let a few in but then he would say, 'Right, that's your lot,' and you just couldn't score against him again after that. He was unbelievable. Pat would unveil his whole repertoire of saves and each carried a hallmark of class. I have no hesitation in describing him as the greatest goalkeeper I have ever seen in the world.

BOXING

The evolution of the cross has created all kinds of problems for keepers. The modern cross is whipped in, bending for the near post, or driven hard to either the near or far post. All of these crosses have targets in mind, with players making prepared runs into the box. The old crosses - floated balls that keepers were able to dominate - are no longer common.

What does that translate to for the keeper? More boxing, or punching of balls.

Don't misinterpret - good keepers still catch more balls than they box - but without question a strong punch is a very valuable tool for a keeper.

A keeper should box (punch) the ball, rather than catch it, when:

- Extreme upper-body pressure, and heavy contact, is about to occur;
- The keeper's first step or two toward the ball is wrong, and now he or she is scrambling to catch up to it, or
- The keeper wants to make a statement. A fist flying past a striker's face or head sends a message - and for sure a more intimidating message than an attempted catch that drops dangerously in the box.

When boxing, do the following:

- Start with elbows and arms comfortably close to the body, which serves as an "anchor spot."
- The actual attack of the ball with the fist is as short a throw as possible. Not a long roundhouse swing - just a simple extension movement of the elbow joint.
- Keep the wrists firm and rigid.
- Keep the thumbs below the surface of the fist - but not tucked under it.
- Box through the low center of the ball.
- Box for - in order - height, distance, width and accuracy. Long, accurate boxes can initiate counterattacks.
- Don't box shots; box crosses.

Here are some boxing tactics:
- Any time the keeper is running forward toward the ball, and opposite to the flight of the ball, box two-handed, in the direction the ball came from. Many near-post crossed balls must be boxed this way, as well as balls flighted into the box from in front.
- When moving forward toward the front post, never try to box across the front of the goal. Box in the direction the ball came from.
- Box one-handed, using the hand closest to the ball (e.g. a keeper moving from right to left would use the right fist). Now the fisted ball will not be boxed back in the direction of the serve, but will be punched to continue in the direction it was originally headed.

General rules for boxing
1. Box for height, distance, width and accuracy (in that order).
2. When moving forward toward a ball served into the goal area, punch with two hands back in the general direction it came from, to a teammate.
3. When moving in a direction away from where the ball was served, box one-handed and in the general direction the ball is heading. Use the hand on the served side. (In other words, if a crossed ball comes in from your right, and is heading for the far post, box with your right hand in the direction it is already moving).
4. Box in traffic when it's likely you'll be bumped, and therefore catching is risky.
5. Punch if you have misjudged the initial flight of the ball, and are working to catch up to it.
6. Punch the low center of the ball.
7. Punch to make a statement to strikers. Strikers hate it when keepers call for the ball, come flying into a crowd, and clear the ball with a strong box just inches from their head.

Finally, I don't suggest boxing for shot handling. Many young keepers do it because they have not developed the finger strength or advanced saving techniques to touch the ball over the goal or around the post.

The following are a couple of simple exercises to reinforce the technique and tactics of boxing.

1. By yourself or a friend, keep the ball in the air by boxing it up. Use both two and one handed techniques and test yourself on how may you can box before it hits the ground.

2. Have someone from the flank toss you balls that require you to move forward in your goal, box it back to them two handed. Now have them toss balls beyond your far shoulder so that you have to move away from the service point and box those balls in the direction they are going. Remember in both circumstances you are going for height, distance, width and accuracy.

3. Now with your team or a few teammates have balls served in from both sides. Don't catch these, box everything just to work on your technique etc. Try to have each box land outside the penalty area in the air. If you are with the teammate goalkeeper, make it a game. Each box that lands outside the penalty area is a point. You can even, using cones, mark off grids from the top of the penalty area around the penalty area to the goal line. The wider the box, the more points. Remember, it must land outside the penalty area.

4. Play boxing volleyball over the goal or over a volleyball net if available or even over a clothes line (get permission first).

Give your time to working on this important skill for keepers and you will find that you have enhanced your ability as an effective goalkeeper. Good luck and remember, play hard and have fun.

"

I had always set short term goals. As I look back, one of those steps or successes led to the next one. When I got cut from the varsity team as a sophomore in high school, I learned something. I never wanted to have that taste in my mouth, that hole in my stomach. So I set a goal of becoming a starter on the varsity…When it happened, I set another goal, a reasonable, manageable goal that I could realistically achieve if I worked hard enough.

Michael Jordan, Chicago Bulls

"

ART OF BOXING

The USA Women's National Team is playing in San Jose before 17,000 fans versus a good England Team. It's the second half and the USA is leading 2-0. England has just earned a corner kick. As the corner kick is bent in towards the goal, USA keeper Tracy Ducar calls and moves towards it. She wins the ball by boxing it towards to the top left of the penalty area. There it is won by teammate Lorrie Fair and the USA starts a 90 yard counterattack that culminates in a spectacular goal by Mia Hamm off a pass by Tiffany Milbrett. I have just described one of the real advantages of boxing a ball. It is a wonderful way to initiate a counterattack.

OK, let's back up just a bit. Yes, the best thing for a keeper to do when challenging for crosses is to catch. No doubt about it, when the ball is securely in the keeper's hands, the attack is over. And yes, it is still possible to initiate a counterattack after catching the ball. There is no argument on either of these points. Catching is better. But, there are still instances that boxing is the safer course of action and there are benefits that can be gained from boxing.

First, when boxing (or punching) a ball, the keeper uses a fist or two fists. No striker likes the feeling of that fist flying by their face to make contact with the ball. Boxing makes a statement, a different statement than catching, but certainly a statement of commitment to reaching the ball and winning it with a physicality that is undisputed.

Second, boxing is the safe choice in the following circumstances:
- When going for the ball, the keeper slightly misjudges the ball and now is scrambling to reach it. It is better to be safe and box than (as often observed) try to catch a ball when out of balance and drop it in front of the goal mouth.
- Often, the flighted ball attracts a crowd. When being bumped or having to fight through a group to reach it, again the safe choice may be to box to clear.
- And, when a certain collision is imminent, boxing will make sure that the ball and you don't end up separated and both on the ground.

And don't forget when the weather is bad. When it's very wet or raining, it's certainly more difficult to catch the ball and boxing may be a better choice.

Thirdly, as mentioned, boxing is an excellent way to start a counterattack.

There are some generals when we think of the technique and tactics of boxing. Always box the low center of the ball and always box for height, distance, width and accuracy, in that order. The height will give you and your teammates time to attack it again. The distance will eliminate the danger. Width will create a better situation if the opponent collects the ball and if you can be accurate then you can give your team possession. Also, even though we make a fist (remember to tuck your thumb below the surface of your fist, but not underneath your fingers), we box with our entire body. We must use a body momentum to generate the impetus which allows our fists to be the final effort and contact area for that whole body momentum. The keeper's anchor their elbows close to their sides and the movement is a simple extension of the arms up through the ball. Never try a round house type of swing. Keep it simple, short compact and powerful.

TIPPING

Goalkeepers must realize that the game of soccer is constantly changing, and they must be able to adapt to its evolution. One area of the game that has immediately impacted the position of the goalkeeper is the utilization of zonal defending and the compactness of team play. Goalkeepers have always been taught to increase their starting position and reduce the angle for the shooter, especially within the defensive third of the field. Now goalkeepers must continue to increase their starting position and work on extending their range while the ball is in the middle and attacking thirds of the field. The goalkeeper has now become a vital part of team defensive shape in a zonal system and must assume tactical responsibilities. As the goalkeeper's defensive line moves forward, the goalkeepers themselves must move forward as well, thus reducing the space behind the defensive line.

Due to the fact the goalkeeper's are now being asked to play farther off their lines, they have become more susceptible over the top. As the play develops through the midfield third and into the goalkeeper's defensive third, attacking teams might attempt to drive balls over the top of the goalkeeper and catch him off guard. Goalkeepers must be students of the game and should be able to visualize different attacking situations they might face throughout a match. As the play develops into his defensive third, a goalkeeper's though process might be:

1. *I must be in a good position to handle any shot taken.*
2. *I must be in a sprinter's stance to intercept a ball played through or a floated cross.*
3. *I must be able to get back to my line and deflect the ball over the top.*

Any number of instances can occur when an attacking team has the ball but as a goalkeeper, handling the floated ball back to the bar is one of the more difficult situations. Dealing with a ball played over the top and back to the bar takes precise timing and accuracy because the goalkeeper needs to make contact with the ball while in mid-flight and the slightest of errors can cause the goalkeeper to knock the ball into the back of the net.

Here are a number of goalkeeping tips for handling balls played back to the bar:

- The goalkeeper needs to start in a sprinter's stance, one foot in front of the other.
- Once the goalkeeper realizes that the ball is played over the top, immediately drop step and move into a crossover step, then into a sprint if needed. It is a race between you and the ball to the goal, and you must win!
- At the last possible moment, leap off your back foot and drive your closest hand to the ball. Time your take off so that you don't jump too early and deflect the ball in yourself.
- When tipping or deflecting the ball over the top of the goal, contact the ball with strong fingertips and with a subtle jab at the ball. DO NOT SWING AT THE BALL, just assist or continue its flight over the crossbar.
- Keep your head steady and focus solely on the center of the ball, where you land and how high you jump should be the last things on your mind.
- Make contact with the ball as you jump up and not on the way down. Deflect first and worry about diving later.

Shots played over the top and back to the bar are rare occurrences in a match, but goalkeepers still need to train this technique to perfection. Many times, goalkeepers can eliminate any risk of balls driven over the top through the appropriate positioning and footwork.

Goalkeepers are called upon to make that special back to the bar save during close range encounters as well. Instances when the attacking team has a restart (free kick or corner) deep in the defensive third can cause the goalkeeper to face the same situation. In this case, the goalkeeper is faced with a close range header or volley from within the 18 that they have to deflect clear and out of danger.

When dealing with balls struck high from close range, the same analysis takes place from the goalkeeper.

Realize you cannot win the cross and immediately drop step to the line.

At the last possible moment, leap off the back foot and deflect the ball over the top on the way upward.

Redirect the ball with strong fingertips and just look to make contact. The slightest of touch could determine the ball's fate.

Training the Back to the Bar technique might be difficult for the goalkeeper, outside of the SoccerPlus environment, due to lack of quality service from a teammate, fellow goalkeeper, or coach. Here are some technical games that you might use at your local training ground:

1 v 1 Over the Top Keeper Wars: Place two goals 18-25 yards apart, with a cone 6-8 yards off the goal line in front of each goal. Goalkeeper #1 starts with the ball in hand, as soon as the opposing goalkeeper #2 sprints to his cone and touches it with their foot, goalkeeper #1 throws or volleys the ball over the top, forcing goalkeeper #2 to deflect over the crossbar. This game can be played with a team of goalkeepers who rotate in after a goal. I would suggest that you start the cone at 6 yards and serve the ball from hands, then progress to an 8 yard cone and volleys.

Crossbar Game: Goalkeeper #1 has a number of balls approximately 40-45 yards away. Goalkeeper #1's role is to work on hand and foot distribution, attempting to hit the crossbar. Goalkeeper #2 starts on the top of the 18. Upon the release of the ball from goalkeeper #1, goalkeeper #2 immediately footworks/sprints back to the bar and prevents the ball from hitting the crossbar or going in the net. Hitting the crossbar is worth 2 points, and scoring a goal is 1 point. After a series of attempts, the goalkeepers switch roles. Once again, I would start with hand distribution from a closer range in order to have success, then simply progress to balls struck from the ground to make it more challenging and realistic.

"

For me, winning isn't something that happens suddenly on the field when the whistle blows and the crowd roars. Winning is something that builds physically and mentally every day that you train and every night that you dream.

Emmitt Smith, Dallas Cowboys

I've always made a total effort, even when the odds seemed totally against me. I never quit trying. I never felt I didn't have a chance to win.

Arnold Palmer

DISTRIBUTION

Everyone knows that the goalkeeper is the final line of defense. But what many people fail to realize is that the keeper is also the **first line of attack.** How many times have we seen a keeper make a tremendous save, then, through poor distribution, turn the ball over to the opposing team? (Answer: too many times!) This not only lowers the confidence level of the keeper; it also affects every teammate's confidence.

Poor distribution skills usually affect young, inexperienced keepers. They fail to read the game properly, and often choose the wrong form of distribution.

As a keeper grows older and gains experience, the ability to read the game increases. Older keepers can see where a properly distributed ball can beat a team. If you can utilize the four main techniques of distribution, you can raise the level of your play **and** your team.

Rules of Distribution

1. When distributing the ball to a teammate, eye contact must be made. This lets the field player know the ball is on the way.
2. If the keeper receives the ball from one side of the field, distribution should be to the opposite side. Most players will be located on the side the ball just came from, so there is a better chance of finding an open player on the opposite side
3. Don't force the ball to a teammate under pressure. Possession may be lost; an injury may even result.
4. Distribution to field players should be toward the ground. If a ball is distributed to a teammate's chest or thigh, valuable time is lost bringing it under control, then moving it down field.
5. Balls should be distributed in front of field players, when they indicate with a forward run. If they go backward and wide, they probably want the ball played directly to their feet. A field player should never have to challenge for the ball on distribution in the defensive third.
6. Practice, practice, practice! That is the only way to improve distribution skills. Once you have mastered the art of distribution, you can raise your game to the next level.

Punting

The following are seven steps goalkeepers can take to improve their punting. Don't try to learn all of these at once. It's good for a goalkeeper to work on one or two. Perfect them and move on to something else.

1) Know the Fundamentals

There are some simple rules that goalkeepers should know and follow when they punt the ball. Like anything else, you have to understand how before you can

improve. The ankle should be locked with the toe pointing down. You should hit the ball with the laces of your shoe. If you hit the ball with the laces and have a good follow through, you will get the greatest distance on your kicks. If you strike the ball lower on your toe, you will not hit the ball on the sweet spot, and the ball will travel lower. The higher on your foot you hit the ball, the higher the ball will travel and you'll get topspin.

Contact should be made even in height to a point just below the knee, and there should be a good follow through. You should land on your kicking foot. If you start too high, the kick will go too high, and you won't get much distance. If you start too low, the kick will go too low.

2) Practice, Practice, Practice

Like any other skill in soccer, punting requires many hours of practice to perfect. It's no secret that the key to improving punts is repetition, repetition, repetition. Goalkeeper trainers can teach the fundamentals and help a player understand the basics of punting, but most of the improvement will be made when the players work by themselves.

The best way to work on punting by yourself is by kicking a ball into a net. While you won't be able to see actual distance, you won't have to chase the balls all over the field, increasing the amount of time you can actually spend on kicking.

3) Create a Ritual

The most important thing a goalkeeper can do to improve punting consistency is to create a ritual. It helps you relax and concentrate. It is very much like when a basketball player takes a foul shot. He goes through a ritual and does the same thing every time. It helps him get into a set routine and enables him to concentrate. Watch many world-class goalkeepers and see what they do just before they punt the ball. It is generally the same each time. They may bounce the ball three times before starting their approach. They may tap the toes of their kicking foot on the ground behind them. They may do a couple of quick squats to loosen up. Whatever you choose to do it is important to do the same things in the same order each time. There should be a purpose to your ritual. In other words, don't develop a ritual just for the sake of doing something.

4) Relax

It is essential to relax before and during your kicks. Don't rush into punts because you will not be able to properly execute the mechanics of the kick. The ritual should help you relax, allowing you to concentrate on the things that are important in punting. To help yourself relax, make taking a deep breath - or anything else that relaxes you - part of your ritual.

5) Drop the Ball with the Correct Hand

If you are right-footed, you should drop the ball with your right hand. If you were to drop the ball with your left hand, you are forcing your body to be in an awkward position, and you will not be able to hit the ball straight on. However if you drop the ball with your right hand, your shoulders are square and your body is facing the field.

A common mistake that young players make is that if they are right footed they drop the ball with their left hand, so they are working against their bodies in an unnatural way. If you are just walking down the street, your left hand moves with your right foot and your right hand moves with your left foot. This is the way it should be with punting too. However, if you are currently dropping the ball with your off-hand and it works for you, don't stop. But chances are good that if you drop the ball with the correct hand, you will improve your consistency and accuracy. There is also nothing wrong with dropping the ball with both hands. In fact, dropping with both hands helps prevent you from leaning to one side when you kick and allows you to come straight through the ball.

6) Don't Swing Around from the Side

To improve consistency and accuracy, you should try to hit the ball straight on, not swing around from the side, pivoting your hips like a field player would when hitting a side-volley. You can still get off good kicks this way. If you hit the sweet spot it will be a good kick, but there are too many miskicks. To develop more consistency, you should try to swing your leg straight through. If you swing from off to the side, you'll get a lot of kicks off to the side, and a lot of duck hooks because you are not getting the part of the foot on the ball that you need. You'll be able to get more acceleration with the leg coming from the side, but your kicks will be inconsistent because you won't hit the sweet spot.

7) Use a Short Backswing
This is a key to good punting. The longer the backswing, the more room there is for errors. So by shortening the backswing, you can increase your chances at effectiveness. The length of the backswing is very important. With a short backswing, you will be able to hit the sweet spot more often and get off good kicks

Dropkick
So you just made a great save. Now what? Your team is behind, and you need to get the ball forward quickly and accurately. The best way to start a counterattack is to do the drop kick. Such kicks, with their lower trajectory (flight path), are easier for your teammates to receive than long, looping punts. The drop kick is also ideal for windy days when you want to kick the ball long but need to keep it low. Remember, a drop kick has a rhythm like a golf swing, and it will take practice to get the right timing. But once you've got that timing down, you can really help your team.

A great way to practice the drop kick is to boot balls into a net standing on the goal line. Listen for a quick "ba-dum" sound when you strike the ball and practice until it sounds the same every time. Keep on kicking, and one day your drop kick might help your team score a goal. And you might even get an assist.

Dropkicking Step by Step
1. The drop kick requires a rhythmic motion. You begin with a windup, holding the ball in both hands. Take a few small steps forward as you move into the kick. Hold the ball with both hands slightly on top of the ball. Lean over so that the ball is in front of you and drop it from just about knee height.
2. Bring your kicking leg all the way back and swing through the kick. Drop the ball straight down beside your nonkicking foot. Plant your nonkicking foot firmly with the toe pointed at your target. The ball and your non-kicking foot should hit the ground at the same time. Keep your eyes on the ball as you release it and keep your head down. Contact the ball with your instep (shoelaces) just an instant after it hits the ground. A good kick will have a quick "ba-dum" sound to it as the ball first hits the ground and then is struck by your foot. Your toe should be pointed down with your ankle locked.
3. Keep your ankle locked throughout and follow through directly at your target. Keep your non-kicking foot planted on the ground. Adjust the height of your

drop-kick by leaning forward or backward as you make contact with the ball. For a longer drop-kick, follow through and land on your kicking foot.

Goal kicks

Too often at the youth level goalkeepers do not take their own goal kicks. The reason is obvious. One of the defenders can kick the ball further. In the short term the team benefits but the costs can be long term to the goalkeeper. Here are some reasons why you should take the kicks.

1) The team loses its defensive shape when a field player has to come back into the box to kick the ball out.
2) The team is a player short when the ball is played out.
3) The opposition can push players further forward because they would be onside.
4) By not taking kicks you will not improve as a kicker. Eventually you will be overlooked in favor of a goalkeeper who can kick.
5) Keepers lead by example. Never get someone else to do your work for you unless you are injured.

How to improve:
- Place the ball on an even surface.
- Strike the ball with your instep (where the laces are on your cleat).
- Non-kicking foot should be level with the ball.
- Use your arms for balance.
- Strike the ball with your toe pointed to the ground and your ankle should be locked.
- Follow through after striking the ball.
- Kick for accuracy whenever possible.
- Keep the ball out of the middle unless your central midfielders are dominant in the air.
- Practice, Practice, Practice!

Other people may not have had high expectations of me… but I had high expectations of me.

Shannon Miller

THROWING

Sling Throw

The sling throw is perfect for distributions of 25 to 30 yards; your throwing range may vary, depending on your age and strength. A sling throw is faster to do than a punt, and it's easier to deliver accurately to a teammate's feet or into space.

1. Cup the ball between your forearm and fingertips and bring your throwing arm behind your body. Point your other arm in the direction of your target, and balance on your back foot. To get more power, run forward a few short steps before reaching this position.
2. With the ball held well behind you, shift your weight to your front foot, and arch your body. Plant your front foot firmly, toe pointed at your target.
3. With the ball still resting on your palm, swing your arm over your head. Keep your elbow locked throughout the throw, and use the muscles of your back and legs to get power.
4. Release the ball with a whipping motion. The ball should roll off your arm, across your palm and off your fingertips. For maximum power and distance, release the ball just as your arm gets above your head. Follow through in the direction of your target. If you follow through high, the ball will sail up. If you follow through low by bending your back, the ball will have a lower flight path.

Bowling

The bowl throw is used for short-distance distribution to nearby backs or midfielders. Use it for throws of up to 20 yards, depending on your strength and skill level.

Make the throw by rolling the ball on the ground, just as you would bowl a ball down an alley. To bowl a "strike," your throw must be accurate, have enough zip to get to your teammate without being intercepted and not be so bouncy that it can't be easily controlled. Try to bowl-throw to your teammate's feet, unless he is running to an open area - in which case you should bowl "to space." With practice, you will develop just the right touch with your throws.

1. Take a few short strides toward your target. If bowling right-handed, plant your left foot and point your toes at your target. Bend your knees to get low to the ground, and bring the ball behind you to waist level.
2. Firmly cup the ball between your hand and your forearm for as much of the throw as possible.
3. Swing your arm forward and release the ball along the ground at the six o'clock position. The lower you get when you bowl, the smoother your roll will be.
4. Follow through in an upward motion toward your target.

"

Show me someone who has done something worthwhile, and I'll show you someone who has overcome adversity.

Lou Holtz

The winners in life think constantly in terms of I can, I will, and I am. Losers, on the other hand, concentrate their walking thoughts on what they should have or would have done, or what they can't do.

Dennis Waitly

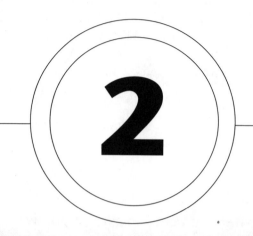

TACTICAL

POSITIONING

Inches, one way or another, make the difference in being in or out of position. Thinking back on a match in my own career, I can remember being scored on because I committed too much to the near post. I knew the striker. Being aware of his dangerous shot, I put myself just inches out of position. Instead of shooting however, he passed the ball across the goal to his teammate who volleyed the ball into the open half. I recovered and actually got a touch on the ball, but committing those important inches to the near post created an opening for the goal to be scored.

Position for the goalkeeper is a continual evaluating, learning and refining process. This is the main reason why goalkeepers are considered to reach their peak in their thirties.

As goalkeeper coaches, we must realize that the quickest way to improve a young keeper is to improve positioning.

The Components of Positions

1. **Location** - simply, where is the keeper in relation to the ball and other players.
2. **Anticipation** - The keeper who reads the game well and can anticipate the next touch (pass, dribble or shot) will generally arrive in the proper position to make the play sooner. An example: The striker receives the ball at the top of the penalty box. As the striker receives the ball, he/she prepares to take the shot. The keeper must pick up on the rhythm of the striker and know exactly when the shot will be hit and therefore time his movements to be in the best possible position when the ball is struck. If he moves too early, the striker will have the opportunity to change his shot. If the keeper moves too late, he will probably be unsettled when the shot is hit and have less chance to save.

Positioning Concepts:

"Ball Line" - The ball line is the imaginary line from the exact center of the goal line to the ball. This "ball line" obviously changes as the ball moves and a sound keeper will continue moving so that his or her positioning is always straddling the "ball line."

When a striker takes a shot, the movement to establish position is almost always straddling the ball line. There are some specific situations, which call for the keeper to be off the ball line, but I'll save those at this time.

"Cutting the Angle" - This certainly should not be a new concept to most keep-

ers and coaches. However, I am amazed at how we can complicate this concept. A goalkeeper will "cut down the angle" by moving off the goal line. The movement is on the "ball line." Really what this movement off the goal line accomplishes is that it makes the goal smaller. Yes, that's correct, by moving off your goal line towards the ball, the keeper makes the goal smaller.

The timing of when to move out and how far to move out is the real test of "cutting the angle."

"The Saving Angle" - Just as cutting the angle makes the goal smaller, the "saving angle" allows for the deflections and touches of the shots taken - resulting in saves and not just good tries.

The ball that is deflected when the keeper is close to the goal line has a much better chance of finding the corners of the goal than the shot that is deflected four, five or six yards from the goal line.

Also, the angle at which the save is attempted gives the keeper a little more advantage. By diving at an angle (and not back toward the goal), the process of making the goal smaller continues right through the save. Another benefit of the angle is that deflections and rebounds will stay in front of you or stay parallel to the goal until they have no possibility of going in.

"The Angle Arc" - An imaginary semi-circle from just outside of one post up to and touching the six-yard line in front of the goal and arcing back to just outside the other post creates the "Angle Arc." This arc is a guide to knowing what the maximum angle is. In other words, the arc serves as a guide for determining how far to come out of goal before actually putting yourself out of position. Remember, I am not talking about a breakaway, I am talking about preparing your position to handle the next touch (pass, dribble or shot).

When the ball is close to the end line and close to the front post, the keeper is positioned just outside the front post. His toes are just beyond the outside edge of the post. The keeper is on the angle arc (maximum angle). To go further out would put him out of position because any ball played into the front of the goal will leave the keeper outside of the posts.

Now, we put the ball in front of the goal, at the top of the penalty area. When the shot is taken, the keeper should be positioned at or near the six-yard line - again on the angle arc imaginary line, again maximum angle and, as we learned earlier, straddling the "ball line." At this point, the keeper has established a balance between being able to react to the shot while still putting pressure on the shooter to try to hit a corner.

Hopefully, the above concepts will be helpful to the keeper and the goal coach for formulating or improving positioning. Remember, the game itself is the best teacher. The more games the keeper plays, the more natural and refined his or her positioning will be.

The following are some exercises that will help you improve your starting position.

Exercise #1: Improving Starting Positions on crossed balls

Cones are placed to indicate the starting position for the keeper and balls are crossed in from both flanks with some balls played directly to goal. Start with a conservative placement of the cones and overextend the goalkeeper to make it difficult to cover balls played directly at goal.

Exercise #2: Improving Starting Positions on through balls

Cones indicating a goal are placed 14 to 16 yards from the goal line. Two sets of balls are placed 35 yards from goal. The server can play a through ball on the ground that the keeper must win before it goes over the imaginary goal line indicated by the two cones. The server can also play a ball directly at goal (driven or chipped) forcing the goalkeeper to utilize a drop step and a side on cross-over step back to the goal line.

Exercise #3: Training the footwork to cover from an extended Position

A server (from hands) positions himself or herself at the top of the penalty area. Two servers are stationed 35 yards from goal and off center. Server #1 tosses a ball so that the goalkeeper must come and catch (or box) it between the six-yard line and the penalty stripe. As soon as the keeper lands, one of the servers out front tries to score (driven or chip shot). The goalkeeper must utilize good footwork to get back to cover his goal.

Coaching Point: The goalkeeper should not hesitate to see where the ball will be played. The keeper must sprint back towards the center of the goal line and adjust to the ball while moving. The footwork is side on cross-over step.

If you set a goal for yourself and are able to achieve it, you have won your race. Your goal can be to come in first, to improve your performance, or just finish the race - it's up to you.

Dave Scott - triathlete

TRAINING GOALKEEPER STARTING POSITIONS

The look of the modern defensive shape is flat and compressed high as far away from the defensive goal line as possible. The reason is that the space in the mid-field for the attacking team to organize the offense is very small. Where is the space? It's behind the defensive restraining line and in front of the goalkeeper. The implications for the goalkeeper are many (footskills, decision-making, organization and positioning.)

The goalkeeper's starting position must be balanced. By balanced, I mean at a place where he minimizes the space between himself and the defense, but also keeps touch with the goal to prevent being chipped.

Let's talk specifically about this position of balance. The ball is in the attacking team's half of midfield. The goalkeeper needs to be between the penalty stripe and the eighteen. This depends on where the defense has established their restraining line. The closer to midfield, the farther from the goal line the keeper must be. It also depends on the pressure on the ball. If there is a lot of pressure on the ball, the keeper can push the defense higher and play farther away from the goal line, but if the ball handler has time to assess the situation and find a dangerous penetrating pass, the defense must give a little and the goalkeeper has to be prepared to cover back to the goal line quickly.

So how do we train for this balanced position? Here are a couple of exercises:

A. Have 2 or 3 goalkeepers alternating on each play. Have a server just above the eighteen and a server about 35 yds from goal (off center is best). The server tosses the ball into the air, the goalkeeper comes from the goal line and boxes the ball high, far, wide and accurately. As soon as the goalkeeper lands and starts back towards the goal line, the server from 35 yds tries to score via a chip or driven shot. As soon as that play is dead, the next keeper goes and so on. The key coaching points are:

1. get back to the goal line side-on (like a baseball outfielder going back for a fly ball). The side-on footwork is a cross over step side on to the ball.
2. go back towards the center of the goal, so that you can adjust to either post.
3. don't wait to see where the shot is going, assume it's going just under the crossbar and get back as quickly as possible.

B. The second exercise puts the 1st server also at the 35 yd line. Also put a cone goal 14 yds out from the goal line. The cone goal should be 10 yds wide. Now either server can side foot a pass towards that cone goal. The goalkeeper must try to beat the ball to the cone goal line and win it breakaway style. As soon as he wins the ball, he gets up and starts back towards the goal line and the other server tries to score with a chip or driven ball.

These exercises work on starting position, the concepts of dominating the penalty area either from flighted balls or through balls on the ground and then the ability to get back and cover behind.

Remember as we improve starting positions and team shape from the goalkeeper position, we must also coach keepers on how to get back to their goal to prevent goals. Good luck!

Pelé on Banks' greatest save:

Jairzinho took the ball in a rush past Cooper, the strong England back, and sent it to me in a perfect high pass. I leaped for it and headed it perfectly towards one corner of the net while Banks, the England goalkeeper was at the other corner. I was already shouting Goooaaalllll ! when Banks, like a salmon leaping up a falls, threw himself in the air and managed to tip the ball so that it slid over the crossbar ! It was, in my opinion, the most spectacular save of the tournament, an impossible play, but Banks made it.

TEAM SHAPE

TEAM DEFENSIVE SHAPE IN THE FINAL THIRD & THE KEEPER'S POSITION

The role of the goalkeeper has changed dramatically in the past few years. With the different shapes of the defense there has been considerable impact on the requirements of the goalkeeper. Let's explore the different defensive shapes and the implications for the goalkeeper.

The Sweeper System: The sweeper system is still one of the most popular defensive systems. The sweeper is designed to solve the breakdowns, taking up sound cover positions for the defenders in front. In the 1995 Women's World Cup most of the teams played with a sweeper system.
The implications for the keeper: The coordination between the sweeper and keeper is vital. The sweeper system has a tendency to spread the game out which is good for attacking soccer, but not so good for defensive play. The keeper will need to use communication and organization to condense the defense whenever possible while not diminishing the role of the sweeper. The nature of balls served into the corners requires the sweeper to move out of the center and once the sweeper is out of the center it is vital that the keeper take over the weak side communication and organization. (See diagram #1)

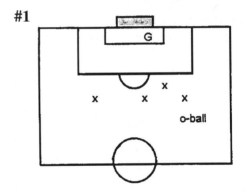

#1

The Flat Back Four: The most common defense played in the 1994 World Cup and a defense that is becoming more and more popular at elite levels around the world is the flat back four. This defense features two central defenders without a sweeper. Because of their flat shape and by using the offside rule, they can condense the space in front of them, in the midfield.
The implications for the keeper: If there is no space in front of the back four, the space is behind. The goalkeeper is responsible for the space between the last defender and the goal and has to make decisions on balls that are played over the defense and whether to come for them or not. Starting positions for the keeper are a key. Also remember that although the keeper is responsible for the space behind the defense, organization and communication are as important as the

starting position. (See diagram #2)

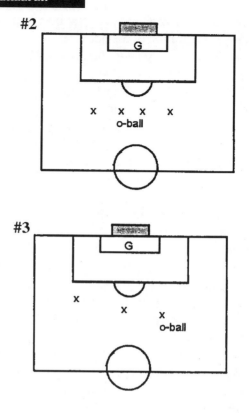

The Diagonal Back Defense: Many defenses in the back 3rd maintain a diagonal look in the back. This means that the side of the defense that is being attacked is condensed while the other side of the defense is giving depth to the defense. The last defender away from the ball is the balancing defender who can still solve breakdowns on the condensed side of the defense.

The implications for the keeper: Because attackers are left onside by the diagonal defender, the keeper must always be ready to win through balls that are well placed to beat the defense. The goalkeeper must always use communication to position the diagonal defender while maintaining depth and some level of condensing at the same time. (See diagram #3)

The 4 Back Defense vs the 3 Back Defense: As mentioned earlier the flat defense is the most common defense among elite teams. To be more specific, the flat back four defense is the most common flat defense. The flat back four allows for the flank midfielders to maintain a slightly more offensive posture because they don't have to balance the defense wide as often. The flat back four also provides for easier possession in the back third and for changing the point of attack with back players.

Implications for the keeper: The 3 back defense requires the goalkeeper to get a bit more involved with possession in the back third. It also requires the weak side organization to be done more often by the goalkeeper because of the spacing difference between 3 or 4 defenders across the back. By playing with 3 in the back, there may be a few more opportunities for the keeper to start a long service counterattack because there probably are more consistently high options to target.

Man to Man vs Zone Defense: In a man to man defense in the back, the defenders will track players across the field and even possibly into the middle third. The advantage is that you can match up a fast defender, for instance, against their fastest striker etc. The downside is that the opponent can dictate your shape in the back by dragging players across the field, thus opening up areas where runs can be made. In zone defense, the matchups are not as easy and the communication and orchestration of the defense is vital. However, your defense maintains a shape that will not only keep them more balanced defensively, but in a better shape in transition to offense.

Implications for the keeper: The keeper in a man to man formation has to be very conscious of runs coming out of midfield and help sort out who tracks or picks up those attacking players. Consequently, keepers with the best communication skills do well because they have the ability to organize beyond the backs and into the midfield. Keepers behind a back zonal organization must be ready to come out quickly on through balls played to well timed runs through the seams of the zone.

Teams that rely on an Offside Trap: An important component of the flat defenses that we are seeing in the modern game is the use of the offside trap. Because they are already flat, it is just a coordinated few steps that puts an attacking opponent offsides. The best defenses do not play offside trap from opening kick-off until the end of the game. It is a defensive tactic that is played for a period of time then taken off. But, for sure, once an attacking team knows the defense is trapping, they are trying to beat that trap with a well timed run and pass and get someone 1v1 with the keeper.

Implications for the Keeper: The keeper must be part of the offside trap. In other words as the defenders step to pull some one off side, the keeper must also step just in case that through ball and run were well enough timed to beat the trap. In this case, the keeper is looking to win that through ball before the attacking player can reach it. Because the keeper will win or challenge for this ball, at times outside of the penalty area, it is important for the goalkeeper to understand the implications of committing a foul outside the penalty area. Usually a foul there is a red card. (See diagram #4)

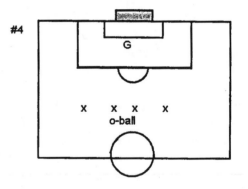

In Summary: We've looked at the modern defenses and some traditional defenses being used in the game today. We've also looked at the role of the keeper and the subtle changes with each defense. We must also identify all the common themes through each defense:

1. Communication: Without question, this is still one of the best skills a keeper can have. When the keeper communicates well (simple, specific, timely), the defense is more organized, less shots are taken, and less goals are suffered.

2. Reading the through pass: A keeper must be able to read the game, understand the best alternatives for the striker and then see which alternative is on and be into the play early to resolve it.

3. Starting position: It not only means extended or away from the goal line. A sound starting position may be in some instances 1 yard from the line, but at other times 20 yards from the goal line. Each keeper must know the tactics involved with starting positions and then know where his personal best starting position is . for each tactical situation.

4. Offensive Player: A goalkeeper must be a good defender, but each keeper must within his abilities offer an offensive possibility for his team, either in possession or with long accurate kicks etc.

❝

The most important thing is to love your sport. Never do it to please someone else. It has to be yours. That is all that will justify the hard work needed to achieve success. Compete against yourself, not others, for that is truly your best competition.

Peggy Fleming, Olympic Skater

BACKPASS

THE BACKPASS, THE KEEPER & THE TEAM

In 1996 when the USA Women beat China in the Gold Medal game, few people would remember that both goals went through USA goalkeeper Briana Scurry. The first goal came after Bri won a dangerous through ball at the top of her penalty area. Her subsequent distribution to Joy Fawcett started a series of passes that led to Kristine Lilly's cross, Mia Hamm's volley and Shannon MacMillan's "put-back" goal.

The second goal was the end of a long series of passes once possession was secured with a backpass from Carla Overbeck to Briana.

The backpass has different personalities. Sometimes it's the last ditch effort of a defender to keep the ball away from a charging striker by playing it back to the keeper and placing the responsibility to relieve pressure with the goalkeeper's soccer ability. Other times it simply means using the keeper as an outfield player to maintain possession of the ball and play through to another teammate.

For the keeper and the team to understand these two scenarios and utilize them with as few mistakes as possible some things need to happen.

A. Communication - mostly from the keeper, but surely within the team. There are four necessary communication commands from the keeper and remember, these in addition to being verbal commands can also be body language, pointing etc. The four commands are:

1. Keeper - this means don't touch it, I will either pick it up if it's in my area or kick it clear if outside the area.

2. Back - this means play the ball back to me. Hopefully to my strong foot. The goalkeeper choices are to one time it up field out of danger or to possess it through a teammate. Dribbling really isn't an option, but if you find yourself having to dribble out of trouble, don't get dispossessed.

3. Away - this means serious trouble, just clear it out of bounds over the touch line and we will organize defensively. Don't give me the ball back.

4. Outside - this means self pass the ball wide and use that touch and better vision to decide what's on for yourself. This is especially a helpful command when the attacker is on the inside shoulder of your defender.

B. Understanding the don'ts of backpassing.

1. Don't backpass once inside the penalty area, just play the ball wide and out of immediate danger.

2. Don't rely totally on information from the keeper, but use it to assist in your decision as a player. However, if the keeper says outside or away, don't give him the ball back.

C. Finally, follow the general rule, Is the risk worth the gain?

Training for Backpasses

The back pass rule was instituted several years ago and most people will agree that it has sped up the game and created more scoring opportunities. However, it is still causing problems for many keepers at all levels. Like any other aspect of the game it needs to be practiced. It is not good enough to play in a 5 v 2 during warm-up and assume your foot skills will improve and therefore you will be comfortable and effective dealing with back passes during a game. Yes a 5 v 2 will help and I do encourage keepers to participate in such exercises but we also need to do more. Here is a way to incorporate training for back passes within a team practice.

1) Coach stands 25 yards out and plays balls into the penalty box. Goalkeeper must clear the ball to one of two target players approximately 40 yards out.

Coaching Points

a) Coach should vary starting point and type of service.

b) GK should strike the ball first time when possible, or make a quality first touch to prepare to play the ball with the second touch.

c) GK needs to communicate with coach as to where the back pass should be played. This can be done verbally or non-verbally (pointing).

2) Same as #1 but add an attacking player to chase coach's pass into the penalty box.

Coaching Points

a) Alternate chasing striker to insure that there is good pressure.

b) Keeper needs to determine when to play first time or if there is time to take a preparation touch.

c) If keeper is under heavy pressure then the ball can be cleared over the touch line. **If in doubt put it out.**

3) Add a second attacker and one defender. Attackers pressure from two sides and defender gives another pass option to the keeper.

Coaching Points

a) Keeper must be aware of weak side attacker especially if a preparation touch is taken.

BACK PASS GAME

What you need:

• 2 goals, 20 cones, 10 scrimmage vests (5 each color), 10 balls.

SET-UP

• Move one goal to the half way line.
• Mark off a new 18 yard penalty box.
• Extend 18 yard line to the touch line

6 v 6 Game

Between the two 18 yard penalty boxes the field players compete 5 v 5. The objective is to make five consecutive passes, one of which must be to the goal-keeper. Field players cannot enter the penalty box until the ball is played in there. At that stage forwards should aggressively pressure the goalkeeper. Once a team has completed 5 passes they may attack the oppositions goal.

Coaching Points

a) Keeper has three options; (i) pass ball to a teammate, (ii) play a long ball over the top, (iii) clear the ball to the safety of the touch line.

b) Communication and decision making points made in the warm up should be reinforced.

Back yard Games for Foot Distribution:

1. Practice your footskills of receiving and passing:

2 v 2 Passing Game

In your back yard create a 3 yard goal with cones or other balls. One team of 2 players are on one side of the goal and the other 2 players are on the other side. You can create boundaries or play without any, it's up to you.

Team 1 serves from their side through the open goal (must serve with the side of the foot.) The ball is received by the other team with one touch and then played back using the inside or the outside of the foot (no insteps) by the teammate. It must go through the goal and now the other team receives with one touch and plays back with one touch. If the ball stops or doesn't get returned through the goal, it's a point for the other team. Each player gets 5 serves in a row, alternate serving teams. After 20 serves, the score determines the winner or create a one serve each tie breaker.

2. <u>Practice goal kicks for distance and accuracy:</u>

2 v 2 or 2 against time

If it's just you and a friend, you can play this against yourselves and the clock. Play for 45 seconds or 1 minute and test your score. If there's a group of you, play in pairs and compete against each other. Here's how it works: Depending on the size of your back yard, get 25 yards apart. Ball starts on the ground and the first pair to 10 wins. Here is how you score. Serve the ball (goal kick) to your teammate 25 yards apart. If she catches it in the air, it's a point. She puts the ball on the ground and serves it back. Count each serve and catch out loud, first team to 10 wins.

Try it again from 30 yards apart. Remember if you catch it inside the 30 yards, no point.

I'm a firm believer in the theory that people only do their best at things that they truly enjoy. It is difficult to excel at something you don't enjoy.

Jack Nicklaus, Golfer

DEALING WITH CROSSES

Goalkeepers are constantly being evaluated on how well they handle crossed balls. The position of a goalkeeper and his role within the team has taken tremendous strides; gone are the days of the shot-stopping keeper who is only called upon when the ball enters the penalty area. If you study how different continental goalkeepers prepare for a match, it is solely dependent upon the league or country's style of play. German goalkeeper's prepare extensively on close range rocket shots from angles while goal-keeper's playing in the English leagues tend to spend the majority of their warm-up on crosses. Different domestic leagues in the world have different styles of play that dictate the goalkeeper's physical and psychological preparation. In the U.S., there is such a vast difference in style amongst teams that American goalkeepers need to be functional in all areas of the game.

The ability of the goalkeeper to 1) make the right decision, 2) improve his starting position, 3) extend his range on balls and 4) dominate that particular area of the box, parallels the success rate of the team. During matches, goalkeepers need to establish themselves, early on, as a dominating force. A goalkeeper's starting position can affect the way the opposition attacks his team. If a goalkeeper is conservative and stays close to the line, then teams will serve balls deep into the attacking third and put the opposing goalkeeper under pressure. On the contrary, a goalkeeper who finds an advantageous starting position, a position that could alter the other team's attack and force the opponent out of their attacking rhythm, is a far better first team choice for the coach. Goalkeepers need to be confident and aggressive while attacking crosses. There is little room for hesitation and no room for self-doubt. Opposing strikers will often test the goalkeeper early with a tough challenge on a cross. If the goalkeeper shows signs of weakness then he is likely to see a lot of crosses during the rest of the game. There is no question that goalkeepers need to be students of the game and need to be able to analyze, evaluate, and anticipate attacking tendencies of their opponent. Goalkeepers must be knowledgeable on the areas of the field that teams are looking to attack.

Catch or Box

How goalkeepers deal with the variety of services faced in a match will determine their team's outcome. The speed and quality of balls served in from the flanks in the modern game forces goalkeepers to have a keen sense of positioning and proper decision-making process. Optimists might argue that goalkeepers should catch all crosses, but realists will debate that some crosses are better dealt with by boxing the ball clear and out of danger. This all-important decision should be made at the last moment. Optimistically, goalkeepers should attack each ball with the aggressive mentality and mindset that they will safely secure the ball; but realistically the decision to box the ball high and wide is a better choice in traffic, under pressure of attackers. When referring to the three danger zones, here are some suggestions to aid in the decision making process if catching is not an option. Remember, " **When in doubt, box it out**."

1. **Early driven cross**, ball played in hard to near post, sometimes behind the defense.
2. **Bending driven cross,** ball curled away from keeper to the 10-12 yard slot.
3. **Floated/Driven cross,** ball played to far post.

#1: The early driven cross requires the goalkeeper to drive the ball back in the direction it came from with a strong two fisted box or possibly a diving single fisted box.
#2: The bending driven cross requires the goalkeeper to box underneath the ball with two fists, using the velocity of the ball to redirect it away from danger. This cross forces the goalkeeper to make contact with the ball under the most pressure from attackers. Goalkeepers also might choose to continue the flight of the ball with a single fist.
#3: The most effective way to deal with the floated/driven cross to the far post is to continue the flight of the ball with a single fist. Just a touch to redirect the ball will offset the attacker who is looking to volley or drive a header.

Starting Position and Extending Your Range

A goalkeeper can eliminate the likelihood of these services based on the correct starting position and angle of approach. How far can I position myself away from my line and still make saves back to the near post and the goal itself? Generally, keepers position themselves one yard off the line and roughly in the center of the goal. But depending on the position of the player with the ball, that might not give the keeper the advantage on a particular crossed ball.

Variables to consider when positioning for crosses:
Distance of the cross
The level of player that he/she will be playing against will dictate a goalkeeper's positioning. At a u-13 level, a player crossing the ball from the touchline will probably not be able to serve the back post area or the center of the goalmouth. Therefore, a keeper could shade his positioning to the near post area. At a collegiate level, a player at that distance may have the ability to serve a dangerous ball thus making the goalkeeper take up a more balanced central position.

Depth (how close is the ball to the goal line)
The deeper a player takes a ball to the goal line, the more a goalkeeper can move away from the line and look to extend range. When a player takes the ball to the end line, the angle for the shot on goal is severely reduced. There is always the chance that the ball will be misplayed and veer toward the goal but extending away from our goal does not mean that all responsibility to the goal is abandoned.

Angle of approach by player crossing the ball
1. If the ball is touched toward the post the striker has the proper body position to shoot at the goal, play a ball into the box on the ground for a teammate, or serve the ball in the air to the back post.
2. If the ball is touched parallel with the sideline, it is much more difficult for the striker to get power and accuracy because he is now kicking across the body. Look for balls to either fall short or be lofted.
3. If the ball is touched toward the sideline, it is very difficult for the striker to serve and the ball will have a tendency to fall short of the near post.

The Early Cross
Balls that are crossed from the flank and from outside the 18 give a goalkeeper the chance to start further off the line (anywhere from 3-6 yards). The shot is still a threat but now the space behind the defense is vulnerable and must be covered by the goalkeeper at every reasonable opportunity.
Factors that dictate what a keeper attempts to win are:
The height of the serve
1) The higher the ball, the more ground a goalkeeper can cover.
2) If a ball is kicked at head height or below, the goalkeeper might elect to hold his position to guard against flicks or deflections.
Pace of the serve
The faster the ball is kicked, the less ground a keeper can cove.
Bend of the serve
1) If a ball is out swinging, the goalkeeper will have to take more steps to get to the ball.

2) If a ball is in swinging, it is basically coming right to the keeper.

Number of players in the immediate area.

Corner kick situations are usually crowded with attacking and defending players. Goalkeepers may have a hard time finding a quick safe path to the ball. On crosses where there are a minimum number of players inside the box, it is much easier to navigate.

Other things to consider

A goalkeeper (or coach) will have to be realistic about what level a goalkeeper should be challenging him/herself. Qualities like quickness, height, power, experience and courage all factor in to where a goalkeeper should be positioned. The process of starting position and range is constantly being adjusted.

It takes years of practice and thousands of repetitions to find that point where a goalkeeper is dealing with crosses further away from goal while not sacrificing the goal itself.

Dominating the Box with Confidence

One of the most important qualities necessary to dominate flighted balls into the penalty area is aggression. Before you get carried away, aggression does have it's down side. Too many of our keepers only play from their aggression. The opposite of aggression for a keeper is patience and sometimes patience is the best way to handle a particular situation.

So what do I mean when I say "aggressive mentality"? Every time a ball is being prepared to be flighted into the box, the goalkeeper should be getting ready to go win it. As it is hit, the first two steps should be aggressive steps towards the ball. These two steps I call "assessment steps". Meaning, in those two steps towards the ball, the keeper makes the decision to continue to go win the ball or realize that the flighted ball is out of their range and return to their starting position, be patient and be ready to attack the next touch. Without question, the goalkeepers that have that aggressive ready to go mentality are, literally, a step ahead when going to win crosses.

There is another side of the aggressive mentality. It's about the keeper playing on their competitive edge. If a keeper only goes for balls that can be caught, they are too conservative. Boxing is an important skill and means to dominate flighted balls into the penalty area. Boxing takes so much pressure off of defenders having to win head balls and when cleared properly (height, distance, width and accuracy) is not only a defensive weapon but often starts a counterattack.

Reading the Game

This is one of the areas that American keepers can improve on the most. By becoming students of the game, one can start to see patterns repeat themselves.

Not exactly, but enough so that a savvy keeper can anticipate the next move by knowing the alternatives of the opponent striker.

A keeper should know each striker's key choices as he approaches the final third and gets in position to flight the ball into the box. This information is important for the keeper to get an early read and an extra step. That extra step factors into the keeper reaching flighted balls or not.

Finally, a coaching point. Don't try to change your style overnight. Sometimes it's just the seed of a concept that will materialize into actual play a season or two down the road. Train and build on the positive while offering a bigger challenge in small doses to reach that final objective. Good luck coaching and keeping.

Finding the appropriate starting position for a goalkeeper is based on trial and error. Focus on positioning and extending range should be addressed in training sessions. Goalkeeper's need to experiment with different positions in order to find the one most suitable for their ability. Kasey Keller found that, in the English Premier League, strikers have the ability to drive balls into the near post at any time and speed, thus forcing Kasey to play more central and closer to the near post. A U12 goalkeeper, on the other hand, can afford to play central but off his line 2-3 yards because his competition usually floats crosses into the box.

Different goalkeepers, different levels of play, and different attacking styles all require different starting positions and goalkeeping abilities. Essentially, there are no secrets to be effective in handling crosses. Similar to math's long division, the more you practice it, the better you become. Evaluating the flight of the ball, securing your timing of take off, and finding your comfortable starting position all come from constant training and repetition. Goalkeepers first need to see a number of crosses from all different angles that are consistent in nature of their competition, then progressing to functional situations with attacking pressure. Our goalkeepers need to handle crosses everyday; the longer goalkeepers go without partaking in crosses, the harder it is for them to regain their confidence, timing, and depth perception. Handling crosses should be incorporated daily, plus it is a great way for goalkeepers to work on their foot distribution and goal kicks as well as the crosses themselves.

THE THREE GOAL SITUATION

The opposing striker beats your left back on the flank, penetrates the 18 and he/she heads for the goal line with the ball. As a goalkeeper, what do you do? What are your priorities as far as positioning? What are you expected to save?

First of all, as a goalkeeper you are expected to save a high percentage of acute angle shots. This is especially true in this tactical situation.

The **"First Goal"** or first priority a keeper must defend is the actual goal itself. Even if there are five wide-open opponents inside your 18, you must not allow the player with the ball to score at the near post. Unfortunately for the keeper, the most uneducated fan of the game knows that a near post goal is almost always the responsibility of the keeper. The starting position is one step in front of the near post and one arm's length away and the body faces the shooter. The position in front of and away from the near post provides a good angle of deflection when balls are driven to the near post and cannot be held. A goalkeeper would much prefer to deflect a ball out for a corner kick than deflect the ball into the goal.

The **"Second Goal"** that the keeper must defend is the space from the near post to roughly the top of the six-yard box. Factors that determine what a goalkeeper can save in this area are:
- The goalkeeper's starting position
- The goalkeeper's technical and physical shot saving ability
- The pace of the ball served
- The height of the serve
- The angle of the serve

The goalkeeper's body must be facing the shot while defending the second goal just as it would be square to a shot that was being taken from the center of the penalty area. The issue here is saving angle. If a goalkeeper is square to a shot that is cut back, his/her ability to attack and intercept the ball is greater. On the contrary, if the goalkeeper positions his/her body at an angle and faces the shot side on, a ball angled back and through the six will be difficult to intercept.

What actually happens is that the keeper ends up diving parallel with the path of the ball and even if he/she can get a hand to it, the ability to catch is reduced and a deflection leaves a perfect central shot for the attacking team. Or, he/she does not even go for the ball at all and ends up giving the opposing team a high percentage finishing chance.

The **"Third Goal"** or third priority when this tactical situation arises, is the space that is at the back post that is vulnerable from chipped balls or for balls cut back into the center out of the savable second goal area.

This last priority is actually the most difficult save. A goalkeeper must normally cover a great deal of ground and be set for the ensuing shot. As it turns out, most shots arising out of this situation are close range/pointblank in nature. For example, the striker gets the ball to the end line and serves a bending, flighted ball to the back post and about six yards out. The goalkeeper must be able to turn, cover about 6-7 yards and get set by the time the shot is taken AND react to the shot. Strategies that keepers use to deal with this situation are:

Use the fastest possible footwork to get across the goalmouth.

In most cases, this will be a sprint. As the ball nears the striker, the keeper must get his/her footwork and body under control and be in a balanced set position for the shot.

Get set and balanced.

It is important that a keeper get set or as close to set as possible, EVEN if he does not feel that he is in the best possible position. By being set, this gives a goalkeeper many more saving options on well hit and miss hit shots alike. The ability to change directions here is paramount. If a goalkeeper does not attempt to get set, a poorly shot ball has the ability to go in and the only chance that a save will be made is if he/she is hit with the ball directly.

How does a keeper know when and where to set? It is basically the same positioning principle as from a shot taken from anywhere else. The keeper must predict where and when the striker and ball are going to meet and then get as close to the ball line as possible. If the ball is going to be shot out of the air or headed, the keeper will need to be a bit more conservative in his vertical positioning and hold closer to the goal line in order to eliminate the looping ball that will fall just under the crossbar. Balls that are played and shot from the ground can be closed down more to increase angle play as the threat from a high looping ball is reduced.

A second example of the third goal situation: The ball is cut back to a player who is central to the goal and about 12 yards out. If the pace or the angle were too much for the keeper to save in the second goal, he will now have to use a crossover step and then use controlled lateral (shuffling) footwork to prepare for the shot. The body should be slightly forward and the hands in a ready position to deal with the shot. At this distance, and with the goalkeeper's angle play, this is now considered a point blank shot (8 yards or closer). The goalkeeper must be able to stand up in the face of such a shot and not flinch or dive out of the way. If the keeper is in a good position and is balanced, he will be able to save a good percentage hit right at him and concede those shots that are well hit and find their way into the side netting.

The great composer does not set to work because he is inspired, but becomes inspired because he is working. Beethoven, Bach, Mozart settled down day after day to the job at hand with as much regularity as an accountant settles down each day to his figures. They didn't waste time waiting for inspiration.
Ernest Newman

SET PIECES

In the 1998 Men's World Cup 43 goals (34%) were scored from set pieces i.e. corner kicks, free kicks and penalties. In the final game Zidane scored two headers from corners. Executing and defending set pieces has never been more important. Not since 1970 when Pelé and Brazil defeated Italy have we seen an open attack oriented World Cup. For better or for worse coaches have scrutinized the game. In many cases even the philosophy has changed. Sometimes it is not the team that scores the most goals but the team that concedes the least that will be successful in the long haul. Brazil, the ambassadors of open attacking soccer, failed to win the World Cup after 1970 until they brought a more defensive oriented team to World Cup USA 1994. They conceded three goals in seven games, defeated Sweden 1-0 in the semi-final, and beat Italy in the final in a penalty shootout. It was a far cry from the attacking flair of Pelé, Rivelino, and Jairzinho.

With the game becoming tighter, it became more important to capitalize on well-rehearsed set pieces. Players such as David Beckham (England) and Roberto Carlos (Brazil) have elevated the skill of taking free kicks to a science. It is a goalkeeper's responsibility to prepare his team for free kicks and corner kicks. Teams will be very creative in devising tactics for these scenarios. However, a well-prepared defense can avert the danger if they remember and employ the basic principles.

FREE-KICKS

A. **From outside scoring range.** *(This distance varies with different levels)*

1. Place one defender in a direct line to the goal ten yards from the ball. This will prevent low driven shots and allows the defender to be in a position to put pressure on the ball when a short free kick is taken.

2. Do not set up a restraining line (i.e. your last defender) deep into the box. Defenders often use the 18-yard box as a guide. This also helps the assistant referee with offside calls. It gives the goalkeeper room to attack long balls flighted into the box, without fighting through players. When the restraining line is too deep, forwards are encouraged to flight a high ball into the goal area to create mayhem.

3. Identify the opposing players who are dangerous in the air, and match up defensive players respectively. All runs must be tracked in and around the 18-yard box.

4. The goalkeeper's starting position should be somewhere near the six yard line, close enough to attack balls over the top of the defense and close enough to the goal line that you cannot get beaten over your head.

B. **From inside scoring range.** *(Direct and Indirect kicks)*

1. Quickly have the pre-assigned players set up a wall 7-8 yards away from the ball. It is best to use midfielders in the wall and let the defenders do the marking. Wall assignments should be set up in practice or in pre-game. i.e. who is in the wall and how many players you need in the wall.

2. Line up the wall so that the outside player is outside the frame of the goal. This must be done quickly so that there is enough time to get set for the shot. It helps if the outside player is tall to prevent high shots into the near corner of the goal. Some teams will use a forward to look at the wall from the front of the goal. This player can make some minor adjustments.

3. On the inside of the wall use a "runner". This player will charge the ball when a short pass is made. Make sure that the "runner" is brave because he will often have to sacrifice his body to block shots.

4. Do not over-focus on the shot. In the Argentina vs England match in France '98, as the English defense prepared for a shot, Javier Zanetti slipped in behind the wall unmarked and scored the equalizer.

5. Ideally the goalkeeper needs to see the ball as the shot is being taken. The optimal position is an extension of the last player on the inside of the wall. Opposing teams often will put one or two of their own players on the end of the wall, thus extending the wall and forcing the goalkeeper across the goal. This tactic adds more chance for a shot to be placed in the near corner. This forces the keeper to crouch down and look through the wall. The goalkeeper's starting position is approximately one yard off the line.

6. Resist the temptation to cheat to one side as the striker approaches the ball. If you guess wrong it is very difficult to change direction quickly.

CORNER KICKS

In 1998 17 goals were scored from corner kicks at the World Cup compared to only 4 in 1994. Services varied from inswingers to outswingers and short services to long balls. The types of defenses seemed to vary from team to team. However, there are some principles that should always be employed to minimize the danger on corner kicks.

1. If the opposing team sends two players to take the kick, two defenders must go outside to contain them.

2. If only one player goes to take the kick then four defenders should immediately take up zonal positions. The first two should take the near and back posts. A third defender stands 3 yards from the endline on the 6-yard box. This player prevents balls being driven low into the box and is also close enough to pressure the ball if an extra attacker comes to take a short corner. A fourth defender (usually a forward) positions himself on the top of the 18-yard box to win any balls that are cleared. The remainder of the players should play a combination of man to man and zone.

3. Look at the role of the defenders on the posts. Their first objective is to clear any crosses that the keeper does not call for or cannot collect. Often the goalkeeper's path to the near post is obstructed by 'heavy traffic' or he is beaten by a near post flick-on which changes the pace and direction of the ball sending it towards the back post. Their second role is to step inside the post on the goal line after the initial cross. By doing this they basically cover one yard each on the line, reducing the goal to six yards for the keeper. When the goalkeeper feels that the immediate danger has passed he will then tell them to push up.

4. Unlike most crosses the goalkeeper is usually under pressure when trying to win the ball in the air. Do not hesitate to box the ball clear if you cannot win the ball comfortably.

5. Finally, look to start the transition offense as soon as you win the ball. Most teams send their defenders forward for corners. If you win the ball cleanly the opportunity to counterattack is on before the opposition can recover and set up.

Ironically, France's third goal in the World Cup final also came from a corner. Except this time they were defending. Upon winning the ball they immediately attacked. Petit broke from the defense creating a numbers up situation and ended the game before Brazil had the chance to get back.

Penalty kicks in regulation time accounted for another 13 goals. See the section on penalties for more information. Meanwhile goalkeepers should be instilling a sense of discipline with their defenders on all free kicks and corners. Concise communication and plenty of practice are necessary so that everybody knows his role.

WORLD CUP PENALTIES

In 1982 West Germany fought back from a 3-1 overtime deficit against France to tie the score at 3-3 and force a penalty shoot out. The game will always be remembered for Schumacher's wild challenge on Battiston outside the box. But it will also be remembered as the first major World Cup game decided on a penalty shoot out. The purists were outraged. Surely there is a better way to determine a winner in a World Cup semi-final. Since 1982 the penalty shoot out has resurfaced in every World Cup and is slowly gaining acceptance as a necessary evil. In 1994 the unthinkable happened. The World Cup Final itself was decided in a shoot out. The purists once again were up in arms. However, by 1998 FIFA had failed to come up with a better alternative and three more countries would be sent home courtesy of a shootout loss.

The Penalty Kick

The soccer penalty is something of a misfit. The game of soccer itself is a free flowing affair between offense and defense. When the ball goes out of play it is quickly returned and the game resumes with little time lost. At no time other than a penalty kick is the game reduced into a one on one duel. It is a team sport. However when a penalty is awarded there is usually a delay of a minute or so before the kick can be taken. It could be compared to a field goal in football but soccer does not have special team players waiting on the bench for such an occurrence. Its closest relation is the penalty shot in ice hockey. But the main difference is the odds of scoring. The hockey goalie has a much better chance of making the save and the skater must execute a series of skills before getting the shot off. (NHL success rate is about 40%) In soccer the kicker is heavily favored and needs to execute only one skill…. kick the ball into the back of the net. This may sound relatively simple but it is not. Since the 1982 World Cup through France '98, 211 penalty kicks were taken and 161 were successful. Simply stated, at the highest level of soccer one out of every four penalties is either missed or saved.

At the 1998 World Cup two second round games(France & Italy, Argentina & England) and a semi final clash (Brazil and Holland) ended up in penalty shootouts. A further 18 penalty kicks were awarded during regulation play, making a total of 46 penalty kicks in the whole tournament. Thirty-seven of the forty-six kicks were scored (80%). The startling thing about this statistic is that the success rate has varied very little since 1982.

1982	77%
1986	77%
1990	73%
1994	75%
1998	80%
Average	76%

Are goalkeepers better now? Are strikers better now? Have their advances nullified each other. Has much time and thought been put into taking or stopping penalty kicks? After they were eliminated by Argentina in a shootout, the English team admitted that Alan Shearer had been the only player to practice penalty kicks in the build up to the game. This is especially surprising since England lost the 1990 World Cup semi final and the 1996 European Championships semi final in penalty shootouts. Italy has fared even worse. In 1990 they were eliminated in the semi final, in 1994 they lost in the final and in 1998 they lost again in the second round. All three defeats came in penalty shootouts. On the other hand, Argentina won their shoot out with England in 1998. In 1990 they lived and died by the penalty. They beat Yugoslavia and Italy in shootout fashion in the quarterfinal and semi final respectively before losing 1-0 to Germany in the final on a Brehme penalty. Since it looks unlikely that FIFA will come up with an alternative it makes sense to take a close look at the execution of penalties at the recent World Cup in France.

How They Shoot

For the purpose of this study penalty kicks have been broken down into three categories. The first is the "push" shot. This shot is played with the inside of the foot by opening up the hips. It tends to be accurate but not powerful. The second is the "driven" shot. The player strikes the ball with the laces of the boot. It is a powerful shot but often the shooter has little idea where the ball will go. The third is the cut shot. This is a combination of the first two. The ball is struck with the instep or on the side of the big toe. When executed properly it can be both accurate and powerful.

The cut shot was by far the most popular. 27 of the 46 kicks (59%) used this technique with an incredible 89% success rate. The push shot was used 14 times with a success rate of 71%. The least popular and least successful was the driven shot. Out of 5 attempts only 3 goals were scored. However, none were saved. Both misses (Mijatovic & DiBiagio) hit the crossbar.

Not surprisingly most of the kicks were taken with the right foot. Ten players (22%) shot with their left foot. There was no difference in the success rate of right foot shots to left foot shots. However, it is worth noting that 70% of left foot shots went to the goalkeeper's left-hand side. 67% of right footed players shot to the goalkeeper's right hand side. Perhaps more significant is an examination of the "cut" shot. Twenty-one right-footed players used this technique resulting in 20 shots going to the goalkeeper's right-hand side (95%). The only exception was Brazil's Emerson who sent the ball up the middle. Five of 6 left footed players shot to the goalkeeper's left hand side.

KEY

🔵 = GOAL

🚫 = MISS

🧤 = SAVE

How the Goalkeepers reacted

The new FIFA rules concerning the goalkeeper's movement along the line seemed to have little effect. Carlos Roa (Arg) shuffled a little on the line but really moved very little. The new rule allows goalkeepers to move freely along the goal-line but it didn't happen. Unlike previous World Cup tournaments goalkeepers tended not to dive early. Most goalkeepers seemed to wait until the striker was almost about to shoot before going in a certain direction. Goalkeepers dove to the correct side on 29 of 46 penalties (63%). In fact, Seaman (Eng) and Roa (Arg) moved the right way on all 12 penalties in their game. Seaman was wrong footed on Ayalla's kick but recovered and was unlucky not to save. It appears that goalkeepers have learned some lessons in recent years. There has been a trend amongst shooters to wait and see which way the keeper is going before taking a shot. In the 80's and early 90's many goalkeepers were already half way across the goal before the shot was taken (remember Jorge Campos against Bulgaria in 1994). As a result shooters adapted their style by delaying their kick and waiting to see what the goalkeeper is doing. In France I believe we came full circle. Goalkeepers waited until the last possible second to dive "early". Ric Miller documented in a previous article (July/August 1996) that 18 of 44 penalties (41%) at the 1994 World Cup were placed in the area 6 feet either side of the goalkeeper. The likelihood of a save in this area is good. However, in 1998 only 5 of 46 penalties (11%) were shot in that area.

Deja Vu

Gabriel Batistuta, Alan Shearer and Roberto Baggio all took two penalties at the 1998 World Cup. Batistuta scored in regulation against both Jamaica and England. He shot once to the left and once to the right. He was substituted before the shootout against England. Alan Shearer took two penalties in that game, one in regulation and one in the shootout. He scored twice with almost identical shots. Roberto Baggio missed the last shot for Italy in the 1994 shootout. With 5 minutes remaining in Italy's opening game of 1998 he stepped up to score the equalizer against Chile and exorcise the demons of 1994. He was called upon again in the second round shootout against France but this time shot first instead of last. He changed directions and sent Barthez the wrong way. Two other participants from the 1994 Final shootout also revisited the penalty spot in 1998. Dunga (Brazil) scored again while Albertini (Italy) missed against France. Suker (Croatia) was asked to retake his penalty against Romania because of an infringement in the box. After checking his pulse he duplicated his first kick to score the only goal of the game. The Romanians are almost as unfortunate as the Italians. In the two previous World Cups they went home after losing shootouts to Ireland and Sweden in 1990 and 1994 respectively.

Which Order

Which order the kicks are taken in a shootout is always an issue of debate amongst coaches and fans. A common school of thought is to use your best shooter for the first kick. This seems to have been the case in the three shootouts at World Cup 1998. Berti (Arg), Shearer (Eng), Ronaldo (Bra), Frank De Boer (Hol), Zidane (Fra) and Baggio (Ita) all converted their team's first kick. Gabriel Batistuta was Argentina's main penalty kick taker but he was substituted before the shootout. After the first kick tactics seemed to differ. Rivaldo (Bra) and Bergkamp (Hol) both scored in the second round of kicks. However, Crespo, Ince, Lizarazu and Albertini all missed. After the second kick the fifth kick is probably the most controversial. The temptation to leave one of your best shooters to last is often overcome by the fear that you might not need a fifth kick. England's Batty was said to have never taken a professional penalty before he missed the decisive fifth against Argentina. The Brazil-Holland shootout was over after four rounds. French captain Laurent Blanc scored their fifth penalty before Italian veteran Luigi Di Biagio crashed his final shot against the crossbar.

Lessons

So what have we learned from the 1998 World Cup penalties. First of all it would be foolish for any team who is considering winning a World Cup to disregard the possibility that they will have to win a penalty shoot out en route to the championship. Germany overcame England in 1990 in the semi final, Brazil defeated Italy in the Final in a shootout in 1994 and France eliminated Italy in the quarter-finals in 1998. Not to mention the US Women's National team outscoring China in last year's Women's World Cup Final. The Italians can only wonder what might have been if they had only been successful from the penalty spot.

The last three World Cup's have each produced a new trend. In 1990 goalkeepers were cheating by picking a side and going early. After the 1990 World Cup many players started hitting powerful shots directly up the middle third of the goal. This trend continued into the 1994 World Cup. In 1998 goalkeepers changed tactics and reverted to waiting until the last moment to commit to one side. Only one ball was blasted straight up the middle and that hit the crossbar. The trend in the mid nineties by players was to approach the ball and wait to see which side the goalkeeper moved. They then placed the ball in the opposite side. By the time of the 1998 World Cup, players had gone back to trying to put the balls in the corners.

Batty, Ronald De Boer and Di Biagio all suffered the misfortune of missing on the biggest stage in the world. It may be small consolation but some of the greatest players in the history of soccer have also failed to convert from the spot at the World Cup. Platini '86, Maradona '90 and Baggio '94 proved that even the greats could miss from the penalty spot.

Summary

The Washington Post conducted an Internet survey after the World Cup and received 1771 responses. They asked how games should be decided in the event of a tie. 16.5 % were in favor of penalty kicks, 71.1% were in favor of playing until the next goal. 12.3% voted for neither. FIFA has not been able to come up with a better solution. As a result nearly every major tournament is resolved in similar fashion. This year the African Nations Cup Final and the Gold Cup both involved penalty shootouts. The 1999 Snickers USYSA National Championship in Florida was decided in a penalty shootout, as were hundreds of other tournaments around the country. Penalty kick shootouts are not popular but they are here to stay.

It's amazing how much of this is mental. Everybody's in good shape. Everybody knows how to ski. Everybody has good equipment. When it really boils down to it, it's who wants it most, and who's the most confident on his skis.

Reggie Crist, Skier

I had never shot over the bar when taking a penalty before in my career. I'd hit the post, shot wide but never skyed a penalty. It was an indication that things weren't right for me. That I wasn't focused. And by that time I was incredibly tired.

Robert Baggio

JD	Player	S/O or Reg	Shot Type	Foot Used	Direction	GK Went	Out-come
1	Collins (Sco) vs Bra	Regulation	Push	Left	Left	Right Way	Scored
2	Baggio (Italy) vs Chile	Regulation	Cut	Right	Left	Right Way	Scored
3	Garcia (Mex) vs Bel	Regulation	Cut	Left	Right	Right Way	Scored
4	Batistuta (Arg) vs Jam	Regulation	Driven	Right	Left	No Move	Scored
5	Herzog (Aus) vs Italy	Regulation	Driven	Left	Right	Wrong Way	Scored
6	Rekdal (Nor) vs Bra	Regulation	Cut	Right	Left	Right Way	Scored
7	Hierro (Spain) vs Buig	Regulation	Push	Right	Right	Wrong Way	Scored
8	Djorkaeff (Fra) vs Den	Regulation	Cut	Right	Left	Right Way	Scored
9	Laudrup (Den) vs Fra	Regulation	push	Right	Right	Wrong Way	Scored
10	Al Jaber (S. Kor) vs SA	Regulation	Cut	Right	Left	Right Way	Scored
11	Al Tunian (S. Kor) vs SA	Regulation	Push	Right	Left	Wrong Way	Scored
12	Bartlett (SA) vs S. Kor	Regulation	Cut	Right	Left	Wrong Way	Scored
13	Souayah (Tun) vs Rom	Regulation	Cut	Right	Left	Right Way	Scored
14	Ronaldo (Bra) vs Chile	Regulation	Push	Right	Right	Right Way	Scored
15	Mijatovic (Yugo) vs Holl	Regulation	Driven	Right	Center	Wrong Way	Crossbar
16	Batistuta (Arg) vs Eng	Regulation	Driven	Right	Left	Right Way	Scored
17	Shearer (Eng) vs Arg	Regulation	Cut	Right	Left	Right Way	Scored
18	Suker (Cro) vs Rom	Regulation	Cut	Left	Right	No Move	Scored
19	Berti (Arg) vs England	S/O	Push	Left	Right	Right Way	Scored
20	Shearer (Eng) vs Arg	S/O	Cut	Right	Left	Right Way	Scored
21	Crespo (Arg) vs Eng	S/O	Push	Right	Right	Right Way	Saved
22	Ince (Eng) vs Arg	S/O	Push	Right	Right	Right Way	Saved
23	Vernon (Arg) vs Eng	S/O	Cut	Right	Left	Right Way	Scored
24	Merson (Eng) vs Arg	S/O	Cut	Right	Left	Right Way	Scored
25	Galardo (Arg) vs Eng	S/O	Cut	Right	Left	Right Way	Scored
26	Owen (Eng) vs Arg	S/O	Cut	Right	Left	Right Way	Scored
27	Ayalla (Arg) vs Eng	S/O	Push	Right	Right	Wrong, but	Scored
28	Batty (Eng) vs Arg	S/O	Cut	Right	Left	Right Way	Saved
29	Ronaldo (Bra) vs Holl	S/O	Cut	Right	Left	Wrong Way	Scored
30	F. De Boer (Holl) vs Bra	S/O	Cut	Left	Left	Right Way	Scored
31	Rivaldo (Bra) vs Holl	S/O	Cut	Left	Right	Wrong Way	Scored
32	Bergkamp (Holl) vs Bra	S/O	Push	Right	Right	Right Way	Scored
33	Emerson (Bra) vs Holl	S/O	Cut	Right	Center	Wrong Way	Scored
34	Cocu (Holl) vs Bra	S/O	Cut	Left	Right	Right Way	Saved
35	Dunga (Bra) vs Holl	S/O	Cut	Right	Left	Right Way	Scored
36	R. DeBoer (Holl) vs Bra	S/O	Push	Right	Left	Right Way	Saved
37	Zidane (Fra) vs Italy	S/O	Cut	Right	Left	Wrong Way	Scored
38	Baggio (Italy) vs Fra	S/O	Push	Right	Right	Wrong Way	Scored
39	Lizarazu (Fra) vs Italy	S/O	Push	Left	Left	Right Way	Saved
40	Albertini (Italy) vs Fra	S/O	Cut	Right	Left	Right Way	Saved
41	Trezeguet (Fra) vs Italy	S/O	Cut	Right	Left	Wrong Way	Scored
42	Costacurta (Italy) vs Fra	S/O	Cut	Right	Left	Right Way	Scored
43	Henry (Fra) vs Italy	S/O	Push	Right	Right	Right Way	Scored
44	Vieri (Italy) vs Fra	S/O	Cut	Left	Right	Right Way	Scored
45	Blanco (Fra) vs Italy	S/O	Cut	Right	Left	Wrong Way	Scored
46	DiBaggio (Italy) vs Fra	S/O	Driven	Right	Center	Wrong Way	Crossbar

PHYSICAL

GOALKEEPER FITNESS

Paul A. Cacolice ATC, CSCS is the conditioning consultant for SoccerPlus camps and operates his company Cacolice Conditioning & Consulting, LLC from Enfield, CT and on the web at http://members.xoom.com/googles1. In addition to 1-on-1 or team conditioning services via mail, email and in-person, Paul has published a book entitled "Comprehensive Conditioning for the Elite Soccer Athlete". More information on his services or this book may be obtained by writing CCC, PO Box 3461, Enfield, CT 06083-3461 or emailing Paul directly at googles@erols.com or googles@netZero.net

Components of Fitness and Importance to Soccer

Fitness can be defined many ways. I prefer to define it by looking at all of the components that can affect the playing of soccer as a goalkeeper. By defining each slight aspect of conditioning as finitely as possible, it becomes easier to see where your weaknesses and strengths are and what areas of fitness need to be worked on.

Below are the fitness component definitions as I see them with their importance to soccer fitness for the goalkeeper.

Aerobic Capacity

Definition:
The ability to perform low intensity work for periods of time from 3 minutes and up. Also defines the ability to recover from activity of 0 to 180 seconds.

Importance to Soccer:
Although very important for the field player, this aspect of conditioning is not as important for the goalkeeper. Rarely does the goalkeeper participate in any activity in the game where he / she must be at full intensity for activity in duration of 3 minutes. This is not to say that it is unimportant for the goalkeeper to have a solid aerobic capacity. This allows for efficient recovery from the small but intense bursts of activity that define a good goalkeeper.

Anaerobic Capacity

Definition:
The ability to perform higher intensity work for periods of time from 0 to 180 seconds. This can also be seen as two separate capacities (0 to 30 seconds and 45 to 120 seconds).

Importance to Soccer:
If anything describes what a goalkeeper is from a fitness perspective, this is it. A goalkeeper must perform all activity in very short bursts of motion, efficiently and at full body capacity. A goalkeeper may not need the longer energy system above

(activity longer than 45 seconds), but any top-notch goalkeeper must be ready to go at full tilt for up to thirty seconds without loss of ability. I could argue that anaerobic capacity is the primary energy delivery system for not just goalkeepers, but all soccer athletes.

Body Composition

Definition:

The assessment of body fat and everything else - ligaments, bones, organs, muscles and tendons. Also necessary in developing the ratio of lean body mass (LBM) versus non lean body mass.

Importance to Soccer:

In soccer, pure strength is not as important as strength to body weight ratio. The higher the ratio will provide more utilizable power. This doesn't mean just getting as thin as possible – as often the strength and power will drop even more than the weight does. Nor does this mean that everyone should bulk up to develop better strength and power. It means finding that balance of maximum strength and power for your body frame.

Flexibility

Definition:

The ease of motion about body joints and segments. Can also be classified into both static flexibility (when body segments are not in motion or very slowly moving) and dynamic flexibility (when body segments are rapidly moving).

Importance to Soccer:

Flexibility is the glue that holds all of the other fitness components together. You cannot have speed without flexibility. Power requires enough range of motion to generate the power. It is also known that the correct stretching of a muscle will cause release of proteins and aid in rebuilding that muscle for the next exercise bout.

Muscular Function

Definition:

Muscular Function is comprised of three components: Muscular Endurance, Strength and Power

Endurance: The ability of a muscle to repetitively contract. This varies from aerobic capacity in that this involves only one muscle or muscle grouping.

Strength: The ability of a muscle to contract against maximal resistance without time limitations.

Power: The ability of a muscle to contract against maximal resistance with time as a factor. Strength over time defines power. The shorter the time (or greater the strength) will increase the power.

Importance to Soccer:

If the arms are driving with power and the legs generate great force, but the trunk fatigues, then the force generated by the extremities is dissipated and lost because of low muscular endurance of the weakest segment. If the arms are required to push a great deal in a very physical game, but fatigue after as few as 100 pushes, then the second half will be turned in the favor of your opponents due to an absence of muscular endurance.

If soccer were played on a field without opponents, you would still need strength to perform vertical leaps, dives, tackles and powerful movements. Against opponents who will attempt to prevent you from performing these activities, strength and more importantly explosive power becomes a serious fitness concern. The greatest importance of soccer strength however, is the amount of power that can be generated with as little body weight as possible.

Orthopedic Integrity/Stability

Definition:

The assessment of the human body's skeletal structure, joint integrity and ability to safely place the stress necessary to train and compete at the level of play you desire.

Importance to Soccer:

Training to succeed at soccer is challenging enough without having to overcome a physical limitation that may or may not be known. Unstable joints decrease the body's ability to transfer generated energy as well as increase the risk for more serious injury. The body is only as strong as its weakest segment. Most medical conditions that can decrease the energy by the human body also can be easily treated and resolved.

Sensory Awareness and Interpretation
Definition

How rapidly and correctly the athlete senses and interprets the environment about him. Soccer specifically relies heavily upon visual and auditory systems for information.

Importance to Soccer:

No player can perform at a high level and make the hundreds of choices in his style of play unless he can accurately assess his environment. Rapid and accurate sensory feedback allows for experience to choose the best decision.

Speed Sub-Components
Definition:

How rapidly the soccer athlete moves from one site to another site. This varies in length of site distances. I like to define soccer as 4 speeds:

* Reaction speed
* First step speed / vertical leap speed
* Five to ten yard speed
* Change of direction speed

Importance to Soccer:

Speed is extremely important to soccer. Most motion for a goalkeeper in a soccer match is performed with speed. Absence of speed doesn't just prevent you from being the best player you can be; it may keep you from being involved in the match itself.

Now, by assessing the fitness areas where you are strong and where you need improvement, you can begin to define what areas of fitness you need to address to become a better goalkeeper. Utilize the list above as a checklist yearly to help you with your progress.

Remember, fitness training doesn't always mean sweating and hurting. Sometimes, working on a skill such as balance may improve your game greatly without giving you a great feeling of a "work-out".

Two to three times per year, it is important to utilize a set series of fitness tests to accurately assess where you stand for each of the fitness areas above. This battery of tests can be one of the most valuable training days of your training year.

Periodization

Initially, most coaches will look upon all of the components of fitness listed above and state something to this effect: That is all well and good, but getting all of those fitness component levels higher (let alone peak at the correct time) will take up too much time. It will leave me with no time to train for soccer. The answer to achieve peaked fitness for all of these components and still leave adequate time for soccer tactical and technical development is periodization.

Periodization is a concept that allows steady gains to be made throughout the course of the conditioning program. The human body will plateau with regard to conditioning after approximately 12 to 14 weeks. For this reason, a program that changes its focus and style of activities before or at that time will allow for more regular fitness gains. The body's natural choice to plateau is believed to be from lack of neurological (nervous system) understimulation. Unfortunately, this may be during the second half of the season or even immediately before the championships. Periodization of a fitness program also allows for timed peaking. Most literature to date has not noted an easily trained peak occurring more than twice per year but the time when the peak occurs can be very specific. Periodization for soccer is very much required as the season can be one very long run (as in most professional soccer leagues) or in many shorter seasons (American premier youth soccer with a fall scholastic season, a winter club season, a spring club season and summer training camps).

Periodization will also allow for training to avoid monotony, make gains and prevent plateaus during your conditioning. Most importantly, with all the fitness variations, getting an athlete to crescendo with all of the fitness components while developing the soccer player is quite achievable.

Below is an example of periodization for the fall collegiate athlete who has very short and limited winter and spring seasons. There are many other periodization models available. They key is to find one that will work to your schedule.

Example:	Periodization for an American Collegiate Player One 3-Month Season, One Peak
Phase I -	**Base training/endurance phase**
Goal	Build conditioning base for future training
Duration	6 to 12 weeks
Flexibility Training	Developmental
Resistance Training	Very high volume and low resistance, specify stabilization muscle groups - scapular, spinal and postural muscles. Emphasis on dumbbell work.
Metabolic Training	Aerobic base development.
Speed Training	High volume and low intensity training with emphasis on reaction and balance development.
Phase II -	**Strength Phase**
Goal	Base strength gains that are not necessarily speed specific
Duration	8 to 12 weeks
Flexibility Training	Developmental in the morning, dynamic pre-workout
Resistance Training	Progress from dumbbell to barbell work
Metabolic Training	Aerobic training on resistance training days, anaerobic

	training on non-resistance training days.
Speed Training	Continue with neurological development such as balance training.

Phase III -   **Power Phase**

Goal	Sport and Speed-specific activities
Duration	8 to 12 weeks
Flexibility Training	Dynamic flexibility daily, developmental on off days
Resistance Training	Olympic-style lifts of high intensity and low volume.
Metabolic Training	Short work intervals at maximal or near-maximal intensity with full recovery intervals - 1:3 work to recovery ratio.
Speed Training	High Intensity and low volume activities.

Phase IV -   **Competition Phase**

Goal	Maintenance of conditioning during the trauma of competition
Duration	Dependent upon length of season
Flexibility Training	Developmental following all activities and day after competitions
	Dynamic prior to all activities
Metabolic Training	Increase intensity of all training to a point less than two weeks before designated competitive season and then taper with skills. Utilize game-duration intervals with full recovery.
Resistance Training	Very low volume and high intensity.

Phase V -   **Post Season Transition**

Goal	Minimize effects of detraining without psychological stress of competition.
Duration	4 to 6 weeks
Training	Recreational games, light unsupervised training.

The Warm-Up and Warm-Down

Unfortunately, many soccer games and practices around the world are uniform in one aspect – too little time and effort are spent properly warming up and warming down. This affects not only the athletes' performance that day, but also their rate of recovery and any subsequent performance for the next several days.

It is noted that the warm-up has several positive effects on performance. Physiologically, the ability to perform exercises improves when body temperatures are increased - usually 102° F. There is also a very strong link between the warm-up and psychological performance. The warm-up is an excellent period to examine individual and team goals, review strategies and become totally prepared for the competition ahead.

A Proper Warm-Up:

- Should progress from general motions to sport-specific motions (general running to soccer-style cutting)
- Warms deep muscle tissue – shown as a light sweat
- Warms joint fluids and lubricates joints
- Increases respiratory rate
- Elevates heart rate and therefore volume of blood flow
  A proper Warm-Down:
- Should begin within 5 to 10 minutes after the end of a training bout or match
- Should digress from sport-specific motions to general motions
- Should be accompanied by 6% glucose beverages
- Should include a meal higher in complex carbohydrates within 2 hours after the end of an exercise bout to aid with faster muscular recovery.

The schedule for the most appropriate warm-up for soccer should follow this course:

1. **General Warm-Up** - Light jog for one-half mile to increase body temperature
2. **General Flexibility** - Developmental Flexibility activities with emphasis on spine musculature, hips, hamstrings and calves
3. **Specific Warm-Up** - Series of short and progressively increasing intensity sprints, with and without ball. Progress to sprints with cutting.
4. **Specific Flexibility** - Dynamic Flexibility activities with emphasis on quads, hip flexors, arm flexors and extensors.

The schedule for the most appropriate warm-down should reverse the above order for the warm-up.

Training for Goalkeeper Specific Skills

Any conditioning program needs to be looked at as a long-term investment in your goalkeeping ability, but the activities on the following pages should be included in your total conditioning program to help you make gains in these specific areas. Your total conditioning program should include flexibility, strength, power, speed and sensory gains to maximize your goalkeeping ability. (ST=Strength, SP=Speed, SE=Sensory, FL=Flexibility)

Training the Breakaway

Ball Drops (SP/SE)
Stay on Feet - No diving!
Create a 5-yard distance between the athlete and partner. The partner holds one tennis ball in each hand with the arms straight out to the sides. The partner drops only one of the tennis balls. As soon as the ball begins to fall, the athlete must react and move to the ball, catching it before it hits the ground a second time. To emphasize staying on your feet, diving is not allowed. Gradually increase the distance. Advanced athletes can be between two partners each with two tennis balls and have only one partner drop one ball to force faster reactions.

Stand with Two Feet on Two Tennis Balls (SP)
Place 2 tennis balls shoulder width apart on the ground. Place the balls of each foot on top of the tennis balls with the heels still in contact with the ground. Bend the knees and hips. Put the arms out for balance. Lift the heels off of the ground and balance. When the heels touch the ground, return to the starting position and repeat. Start out with attempting a 15-second continuous balance as a goal. An excellent level would be anything greater than 30 seconds (In excess of 2 minutes is not unheard of).

Bear Crawl (ST/SP)
From the end-line to the 18-yard box, crawl on all fours (knees and hands). The key is to bring the knee forcefully forward with each step (this is what happens with an effective first step or vertical leap). This can be made more challenging by having the partner hold the ankles so that lifting the knee forward is more difficult. Races are excellent for this activity.

Dead Lifts (ST)
Before you begin, the barbell is evenly loaded with collars secured and the floor is padded and clear. You should wear a weight belt with the wide part over your abdomen (buckle in back).

To start, the spine is straight and kept straight throughout the entire activity. The hands are placed on the bar with a one overhand (pronated) and one under (supinated) grip. The knees and hips are bent. Feet remain flat on the floor at all times. Head faces forward throughout the motion. (This starting position should look like a baseball catcher beginning to stand up out of a stance).

Begin to lift the bar by first contracting the buttocks, tucking the hips and lifting with the legs. Come to a standing position by slightly arching your spine backwards. If the resistance is correct, your perceived "arching" will actually maintain the spine in a straightened position.

The descent is a reverse performance of the ascent. Special emphasis is placed on keeping the spine in an upright position until the bar is safely on the floor. The legs perform all moving work. The spine simply stabilizes.

Training for Distribution

Shoulder Arc Walks (ST)/SP)
In a push-up position, the athlete walks to the right and left while keeping the feet in one place. Doing this activity forces the athlete to walk in a circle with the arms. Have the partner walk around the athlete's circle, first slowly and then increasing the speed, while the athlete attempts to walk with their arms so that their head stays facing the partner's knees. As the speed of the partner increases, have the partner also rapidly change directions as he walks.

Push-Up with a Plus with a Wide Grip (ST)
In a straight body position, place the partner's fist underneath the athlete's breastbone (middle of the chest). Perform a push-up so that the athlete's mid chest contacts the partner's fist and then pushes up so that the arms are straight and locked. The hands should be 1 1/2 times as wide as the shoulders. Then push the chest up even further by shoulder shrugging forward so that the shoulder blades begin to move forward. This second movement is very small and must be done with the body still rigidly locked from shoulders to ankle.

Seated Dips (ST)
With the athlete's feet on a ball, place hands on the edge of a bench or first row of bleachers. The athlete takes a straight leg seated position in between the ball and the bench. Making sure that the shoulders do not rise to the ears, the athlete allows the elbows to bend and the buttocks to drop almost to the ground without touching. The arms are then straightened. Repeat.

Height Skipping (SP)
Utilizing a skipping motion, attempt to maximize hang time in the air while achieving maximal height for each skip. It is very important to utilize the arms for assistance.

Eye Tracing (SE)
Take a poster board and randomly draw 2 inch tall numbers in no order over the card. I like to draw the numbers 0-100 on a two foot by three-foot board. Place a star around the number 0 and with your eyes only; track a path in numerical order. If the board is designed well enough, the eyes will be forced to move all over the board increasing the span as well as the speed of number recognition.

Training to Tip and Parry

Hand-Eye Coordination/Swinging Ball (SE)

Take an old tennis ball and drill a hole through the center. Place a 12-foot long string through the center and knot so that the tennis ball sits at the end of the string. Place the tennis ball over the goal crossbar and secure so that the ball swings freely about 2 feet off of the ground.

Move the ball so it begins to swing. Take either foot and attempt to follow the ball's path closely without touching the ball. Stand in one place while doing the skills initially. Sit down on the ground and do the same thing. Goalkeeper or not, everyone utilizes their hands to benefit their positioning in this sport. Then do the same thing tracking the ball with your thigh, elbow and down the limbs back to the body. Finally, track the ball with your head. Every time your head moves, your eyeballs get wiggled slightly. This instantaneously throws off your acuity. The best visual athletes rapidly refocus on an object and continue with play.

Fast Hands / Fast Feet (SP)

Standing in place on one leg with the other leg's knee slightly bent, heel in the air and toes touching the ground, tap one toe against the floor as many times as possible in 10 seconds. Repeat with the opposite foot. Repeat with each foot for 20 and then 30 seconds.

Place the palms of the hands lightly against any solid object (or even a partner's shoulders). Rapidly tap all of the fingers of one hand at once on the object as many times as possible in 10 seconds. Repeat with the opposite hand. Repeat with each hand for 20 and then 30 seconds.

Push-Up with a Plus with a Narrow Grip (ST)

In a straight body position, place the partner's fist underneath the athlete's breastbone (middle of the chest). Perform a push-up so that the athlete's mid chest contacts the partner's fist and then pushes up so that the arms are straight and locked. The hands should be even with the shoulders. Then push the chest up even further by shoulder shrugging forward so that the shoulder blades begin to move forward. This second movement is very small and must be done with the body still rigidly locked from shoulders to ankle.

3 Way Scapular Stabilization (ST)

With surgical tubing attached to a solid and non-moving object at the mid-point of the tubing, the following activities are performed:

Rhomboids: The athlete faces the tubing with one end in each hand. Keeping the spine upright and in neutral position, the athlete brings the arms, palm down, to the side of the rib cage. This forces the shoulder blades to pinch over the spine.

Latissimus: The athlete faces the tubing with one end in each hand, keeping the spine upright and in neutral position. The athlete starts with the thumbs skyward, and while bringing the arms to the hips, turn the hands to a thumbs back position. This maximizes the contraction of the latissimus, which is an important shoulder stabilizer.

Serratus Anterior: The athlete faces away from the tubing with one end in each hand. The athlete keeps each arm locked straight in front. Keeping the chest in place, the arms are pressed further forward (by rolling the shoulder blades further forward) as if to touch an object 4 inches away. Relax the shoulder blades but not the arm, elbows or spine and repeat.

Superman Exercise (ST/FL)

Lying on the ground upon your spine, lift the entire left arm and the entire right leg off of the ground as though you were flying through the air. It is important that you do not twist at the spine to accomplish this task. Hold for 5 seconds. Alternate arm/leg and repeat.

"

My father taught me that the only way you can make good at anything is to practice and then practice some more. It's easy to practice something that you are good at, and that's what most people do. What's tough is to go out and work hard on the things you don't do very well.

Pete Rose

I never stay away from workouts. I work hard. I've tried to take care of my body. I'll never look back and say that I could have done more. I've paid the price in practice, but I know I get the most out of my ability.

Carl Yastrzemski, Boston Red Sox

GOALKEEPER NUTRITION

To optimize nutrition, first, get to know and regularly work with a knowledgeable dietitian or nutritionist who knows sports in your immediate area. There is information available which will greatly affect your performance. I stress that all nutritionists or dietitians who I refer to must either still be active in sports or have an extensive background in sports. This is for a reason. If all you had to do in life was monitor closely what you consume and with an unlimited budget, then you could be the most efficient in your food choices. This is difficult to do however.

Anaerobic sports (such as soccer) utilize more fuel from glycogen, not fat. Glycogen is derived from complex carbohydrates such as whole wheat breads, cereals, pasta, fruit, vegetables, and potatoes. Such sources of carbohydrates (and glycogen) are important before activity and must be replenished as soon as possible after activity.

Be aware of any nutrition plan that greatly emphasizes pre-made meals. That is a great scenario for the off-season when you have the time to follow these guidelines, but as an athlete, your focus should be on other aspects of your training.

Be aware of nutrition guidelines that are primarily supplement-based. What the human body requires can be gotten in food items. It has been that way since time began for our species. There are many food components that can be absorbed most effectively when in certain combinations (calcium is one such chemical). These combinations occur in nature. It is difficult to overdose on any chemical when obtaining them through the diet, while much easier to overdose when taking them in supplement form.

Be aware of food intakes. Write down everything that you consume for one entire week. Yes, everything (Water, snacks, all meals including deserts). It is quite an awakening experience.

Pre-Game and Pre-Practice Meals

Being properly glycogen-loaded is as important to sports such as soccer as a Formula 1 car driver having a full tank of the right kind of fuel. A pit crew chief just has to check the amount of fuel left on the fuel gauge. However, for the human machine, I do not think that anyone has developed a method to place a glycogen gauge anywhere on the human body.

Properly glycogen-loaded athletes will be 3 to 4 pounds heavier, because glycogen cannot be stored without also storing water. This is the easiest method to get a rough gauge on how well the body is prepared for higher anaerobic sports such as soccer.

To increase glycogen stores, look to consume slowly digested carbohydrates with low glycemic effect (small rush of blood sugars) – see chart. These would be apples, fruit yogurt, skim milk, lentils, and dried apricots. Look NOT to consume slowly digested carbohydrates with high glycemic effect (greater rush of blood sugars) Examples of these would be baked potatoes, honey, maple syrup, white bread and Cheerios

Don't utilize the day of a game to try a new food type that may or may not agree with you. Always try any new item when your body has the time to reject it (if that happens) without affecting your performance.

Post-Game and Post-Practice Meals

After hard exercise, the body needs to consume easily digested sugars to begin rebuilding the body. As a general rule, look to consume 0.5 grams of carbohydrates/pound body weight. This would mean that a 150 pound athlete eats 75 grams of carbohydrates and a 100-pound athlete eats 50 grams of carbohydrates. For reference, 8 ounces of apple juice contains 30 grams of carbohydrates, large banana 40 grams and medium bagel 50 grams.

Look to consume rapidly digested carbohydrates with high glycemic effect (greater rush of blood sugars). These would be baked potatoes, honey, maple syrup, white bread and Cheerios.

Attempt to consume a solid meal of these carbohydrates within 2 hours of the end of a practice or an event. If you have difficulty eating a solid meal during this time, try to use a liquid meal (see below) within 30 minutes after an event or practice to replenish carbohydrates and begin the recovery process even faster.

Glycemic Index for Foods

As was mentioned earlier, the rate of breakdown and release of sugar into the body is known as the glycemic effect. The more rapidly the foods digest, the higher the glycemic effect. Here is a very partial list of low, moderate and high glycemic effect foods.

Low Glycemic Effect	Moderate Glycemic Effect	High Glycemic Effect
Apple	Apple Juice	Bagel
Banana - Under-ripe	Baked Beans	Baked Potato
Grapefruit	Banana - Ripe	Bread
Kidney beans	Bran Chex	Cereals -Most Non-Bran
Low-fat Yogurt	Corn	Corn Flakes
Milk	Green Peas	Gatorade
Pear	Lentil Soup	Graham Crackers
	Orange	Honey
	Orange Juice	Oatmeal
	Popcorn	Watermelon
	Rice	Raisins
	Spagetti without sauce	Rice Cakes
		Wheat Thins
		Vanilla Waffers

A Quick Answer to "Feed the Need"

The more rapidly the body can intake energy, the faster that recovery from activity can take place. If you are like myself, eating immediately after a match can be a difficult experience, but one which will greatly increase the recovery rate. This can be even more important while playing multiple, high-intensity games such as a tournament.

Author Nancy Clark suggests an answer to this problem may be found in "liquid" meals. Research has shown that the same food components are digested and tolerated much faster when blended into a liquid.

She suggests two sample (and simple) liquid meals for immediately after or a little before a game when a solid meal would be too much to handle.

Liquid Meal Suggestions

Cereal Shake: (450 kcal; 60% CHO, 20% Protein, 20% Fat)
2 cups low fat milk
1 cup cereal
1 small banana
4 cups ice OR 1 cup vanilla yogurt
Blend and drink. Try different cereals and fruit combinations that best suit your taste buds!

Fruit Shake: (470kcal; 75% CHO, 15% Protein, 10% Fat)
1 cup vanilla yogurt
4-6 peach halves
4 graham cracker squares
Blend and drink.

Planning Your Meals

The only thing more important than what you eat is making sure that you have planned the right time to eat the correct things. Below is a handy schedule of good food strategies for optimum performance.

Practice eating behaviors and items before game time. Your body may not adjust well to something and right before a big event is NOT the right time to find this out. Practice these skills in pre-season when you have the time to assess your body's reaction to these foods and practices.

Be aware of how long it takes for certain foods to digest. Here is where faster recovery from games comes in. As far as macronutrients go, the times are below. Remember; don't attempt to consume a roast beef or chicken sandwich with three hours to go before a match. Think about these numbers before planning a pre-match meal. Ideally, a meal the morning of an evening match can be mixed among those below, but realize that a complex carbohydrate meal such as baked potatoes, salad, pancakes or pasta (watch the fatty sauce) helps prep the muscles better.

Proteins: 6 to 8 hours

Simple Carbohydrates: 1 to 2 hours
Complex Carbohydrates: 4 to 6 hours

When	Good Strategy is to:
48 Hours Before a Game or Practice	Correct any hydration problems - avoid any beverages that cause dehydration (any caffeinated beverages including coffee, colas) Plan your meals for the 24 hours prior to the game/practice
24 Hours Before a Game or Practice	Consume meals that have low glycemic effect to maximize the glycogen that your body can store. Continue to consume fluids until your urine is clear and odorless.
Day of a Game or Practice	For an evening event, a hefty, hearty high carbohydrate breakfast and lunch with low to moderate glycemic effect foods. A lighter meal can be consumed 2 - 2 1/2 hours before a game. Maintain good hydration
30 Minutes After a Game or Practice	Carbohydrate-heavy beverage (such as liquid meal) with at least 1-2 pints of replacement fluids to aid with rapid recovery.
2 Hours After a Game or Practice	Solid meal with high glycemic effect foods (great for the bus trip home) with up to a quart of a sports drink.

Recovery from any match can be aided with intelligent food choices. This matters not only for what you eat, but when. It is known that input of a higher carbohydrate meal within 30 minutes after the end of a match will aid recovery. Usually, you cannot eat solid food within 30 minutes after a match, so athletes I work with consume "liquid meals" of yogurt, cold breakfast cereal and fruit blended in a mixer. Then a solid meal is consumed as soon as possible and ideally within 2 hours after the end of the match. The liquid meal provides various carbohydrates without bloating.

Fluid Intake Schedule
Get enough fluid. When you are thirsty, you are already at least 1 pint low on

fluid. Fluid has many effects on your body. It cools you, it keeps your joints lubricated, but it also allows the muscles and nerves to contract and even allows you to think. Being dehydrated usually affects your ability to even know you are dehydrated! Begin with small sips of fluid early and often in your training session. Cold fluid works best.

When it comes to choice of fluid, there is still debate as to what is the best choice. The number one factor is how fast fluid is absorbed into the body. This is usually done in the stomach. Water is an excellent choice when in doubt. There is some evidence that a slight increase in some electrolytes may actually increase fluid absorption rate. It is accepted that an increase in sugars will also benefit extended athletic performance. The amount of all sugars needs to be low (at or below 6%) unless the sugars have been chemically modified to be broken down easily. Most sports drinks vary around the above limits and for most single game soccer activities, do not really significantly and negatively affect athletic performance. Multiple games within a day such as in a tournament demand intelligent fluid intake among other strategies.

Cold fluid does not give you cramps. Chugging fluid does! The amount of water your stomach can absorb at one time is small, but steady. Sipping fluid allows water to be absorbed without cramping. Even cold fluid! That's why I train with a bicycle-style water bottle that doesn't allow me to chug. Think about having 2 bicycle-style water bottles when you train as they each hold only one-half of the water that you need.

Highly Advised Reference
Clark N, Sports Nutrition Guidebook: Eating to Fuel Your Active Lifestyle, Leisure Press: Champaign, IL, 1990.

Here is a schedule to address fluid consumption before and after an event.

Event	Fluid Goals
2 hours before event (practice or game)	16 to 24 ounces intake
15 minutes before event	8 to 16 ounces intake
Every 15 to 20 minutes during event	6 to 8 ounces intake
After activity	Look for pale and colorless urine
Daily normal intake	Look to have to urinate every 2 to 4 hours

GOALKEEPER FOOTWORK

Training Objective: To increase GOALKEEPER SPEED;
reaction speed, 1st step, change of direction, and 5-10 yard stride speed.

Training Session #1: Goalkeeping Explosive Footwork
(End cones are 6-8 yards apart)

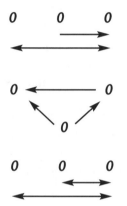

1. <u>Lateral footwork:</u> face middle cone, turn & sprint to cone #1, then sprint to #2, then #3. (Alternate directions each time)

2. <u>Triangle footwork:</u> backwards, side shuffle, sprint backwards, crossover, sprint (change directions)

3. <u>3-cone footwork:</u> lateral shuffle short/short/long;
Linear short/short/long (forwards, backwards run)
Shuffle short/short and sprint long

Training session #2: Goalkeeper Box footwork

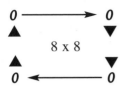

Warm-up: Two keepers, start at different corners.
1. Jog, high knees, jog, high knees 8 x 8
2. Jog, cariocca, jog, cariocca
3. Backwards, shuffle, backwards, shuffle
4. Skip, shuffle, skip, shuffle

Training exercises:

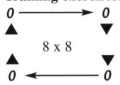

1. Sprint forward
2. Crossover step
3. Backpedal
4. Crossover

1. Sprint forward
2. Backpedal
3. Crossover
(repeat other side)

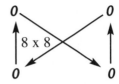

1. Sprint forward
2. Diagonal crossover
3. Sprint forward
4. Diagonal crossover

Training session #3: Goalkeeper Bounding/Jumping
Distance covered 18 yards, recovery jog back to start
1. Right foot jump
2. Left foot jump
3. Power skipping
4. High knee running
5. Bounding
(land and jump off of same foot)

6. Semi squat jumping (legs 90*deg.)
7. Double leg jumps (2)....sprint
8. Push up position...........sprint
9. Sprint
10. Lunges

OR (more advanced training exercises.)

1. Walk with hands on head, driving the knee to the shoulder
2. Running man power skip, driving the arms and leg simultaneously
3. Drive knee up and out, and back down…..into a skipping motion
4. Side lunges in a squat position
5. Backwards running driving leg up and out
6. Split stance jumping forward
7. Resistance sprinting…….resist from the front (sprinter pushes on shoulders)
8. Resistance sprinting…….resist from the back (pull on shirt tail)

Training session #4: Goalkeeper Sprint Conditioning:

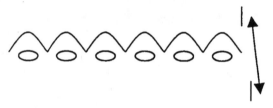

4 yards   8 yards   Total = 12 yards

Training variations:
(concentration lies on transfer of weight and 1st step into sprint.)
1. Jog 1st 4 yards, sprint 8 yards
2. Left and right footed quick hops,
sprint 8 yards
3. Double knee jumps (for height/power), sprint
4. Jog forward to 1st cone, backpedal quickly…on command of go, sprint
5. Backpedal 4 yards, turn and sprint
6. Start on stomach, up and sprint
7. Start on back, turn, up, and sprint
8. Start in a push up position, drive foot forward and sprint

Training session #5: Goalkeeper Cone Footwork:
(Focus is on quickness/agility.)

Training exercises: (3x/keeper)
These exercises can be two sessions (footwork/jumping.)
1. Double touches, quick feet through cones, lateral shuffle right/left
2. Double touches side on (facing one direction), forward sprint and backpedal
• *Alternate sides*
3. Single touches, quick feet, lateral shuffle
4. Single touches, high knees, lateral shuffle
5. Double touches, up one cone, back one cone, lateral shuffle
6. Double knee jumps over cone (for height), lateral shuffle
7. Double knee jumps side on, backpedal and forward sprint
• *Alternate sides*
8. Left/right footed jumps, lateral shuffle
9. Bounding over cones (land and jump off same foot), lateral shuffle

Training session #6: Goalkeeper Jumping:
(use lines of cones or flags/poles)

Training exercises:
1. High knees, jog, high knees, jog, high knees
2. Double knee jumps, high knees, double knee jumps
3. Double touches (quick feet), double knee jumps, double touches
4. Mogul style jumping (2 footed w/ a twist), high knees, double knee jumps
5. Any jumping/footwork variations

Training session #7: Goalkeeper Coordination:
(Focus lies on transition and 1st step.)

10 yards	10 yards	10 yards

1. Quick feet   skip   _ sprint
2. High knees   jog   _ sprint
3. Jog   high knees   _ sprint
4. Left footed hops......sprint 20 yards (repeat with right foot)
5. Skip   sprint.............................
6. Any jumping/footwork variations

Training session #8: Goalkeeper Fitness:

18 yards

Partner runs: 1st goalkeeper sprints (with ball in hands) 18 yards and back, 2nd goalkeeper runs alongside to pace, when they get back to the start the 3rd goalkeeper paces the 1st goalkeeper. Then 2nd goalkeeper runs solo, and 3rd goalkeeper paces, then 1st goalkeeper runs with them. 3rd goalkeeper repeats the sequence.

OR

Goalkeeping sprint shuttle runs with cones at:

6 yards,   12 yards,   18 yards.

0   0   0   0

Good footwork is necessary to make flying extension saves.

MEDICINE BALL TRAINING

The KwikGoal / SoccerPlus medicine ball is a training tool that no goalkeeper or goalkeeper coach should be without. When used properly, this weighted ball will significantly improve areas of goalkeeping such as catching and throwing. The med ball can be used as a substitute to a regular ball in almost any exercise where the ball is thrown or volleyed.

The greatest benefit of training with a medicine ball is that it immediately exposes technical weaknesses. Therefore it is a great tool when training goalkeepers in technical skills such as catching, diving, throwing etc. The mere weight of the ball will make it difficult to hold if the technique is not correct. The following are some common technical problems that are regularly exposed by the medicine ball.

Basket catching
If the arms and elbows are not parallel and close together the ball will squirm free near the elbow area. The body should be relaxed and slightly bent to absorb the impact of the ball. If the upper body is upright and rigid the ball will bounce out.

Contour/high contour catching
Hands cannot be too close together. If they are they will not cover enough surface of the ball. If the fingers do not make contact with the ball first the ball will rebound off the palms. The worst scenario is when the hands are too far apart. In this case the medicine ball will go straight through the hands and either go in to the goal or hit the keeper in the face or head.

Side contour/Collapse diving
One of the main components of the collapse dive is to move forwards and catch the ball in front of you. The medicine ball will try to force the hands backwards. By resisting the medicine ball the hands become stronger. After catching the ball in a collapse dive it must now be taken to the ground. Again because of its weight the medicine ball is harder to pin to the ground. Many repetitions will develop the arm strength and balance to perform this task effectively.

Throwing
After each save the goalkeeper should distribute the ball by hand back to the coach. The medicine ball will improve throwing greatly. The keeper will need to have a better grip on the ball and follow through after the release. Because the medicine ball is heavier the keeper will improve arm strength as well as technique.

No training session should comprise solely of medicine ball work. It is important to also use a regular ball for several reasons. First of all we play with regulation weight balls so that is the ball we need to handle most. Secondly, a regulation ball will feel real good after using a medicine ball for twenty minutes. Psychologically the keeper will feel a lot stronger. It will seem a lot easier to catch a regulation ball and as a result confidence levels will rise. Some goalkeepers will use the medicine ball as part of their pre-game warm up for this reason.

The KwikGoal / SoccerPlus Medicine Ball weighs 2lbs. This may not sound like a lot of weight but after catching for 15 to 20 minutes you will start to feel the extra weight. This introduces another benefit, strength training. Those keepers who use the ball on a regular basis will attest to an increase in strength in their hands, wrists, and arms. With regular and proper use of the KwikGoal Medicine Ball, I guarantee there will be increased catching percentage, upper body and arm strength and most of all, a greater confidence in the goalkeeper's own ability to deal with and consistently hold onto difficult shots.

CAUTION: *The med ball should never be kicked from the ground. Only coaches with the technical ability and strength should half volley the ball. Age 13 is usually a good time to introduce the ball to your goalkeepers' training sessions.*

Former England World Cup Goalkeeper Peter Bonetti trains SoccerPlus students with the medicine ball.

MINI BALL TRAINING

As coaches, whether it be specifically for goalkeepers or field players, we are constantly searching for new innovative ways to train our players. Especially when dealing with goalkeepers, coaches need to train and put them through a series of exercises that will prepare them for the complex and variety of situations the goalkeepers will face between the sticks. Many experienced goalkeeper coaches have already begun using innovative training methods that will maximize their goalkeeper's potential. **Mini ball training** is one way in which coaches can help prepare their goalkeepers for the demanding position.

At SoccerPlus Goalkeeper School, directors and staff coaches use Size 2 mini balls in a series of shot handling exercises. The coaches are looking to acquire an optimal level of goalkeeping from the campers. The primary goalkeeping skill attributed to the mini ball training is the adjustment of the catching unit, or the contour catch. With the flight of a Size 2 soccer ball, the goalkeeper needs to adjust his hand position from a Size 4 or 5 to a much smaller, precise catching position. Securing the ball with an appropriate catching unit requires more than a safe pair of hands. The involvement of the goalkeeper's upper body is equally important, specifically the head and chest. Goalkeepers need to prepare their bodies so that their hands, head and chest are in alignment with the ball.

The secondary skill acquired by the use of mini ball training is an increase in physical and visual reaction speed. Obviously the use of a smaller ball, whose flight will be rapid, will require the goalkeepers to prepare their feet quicker in order to save. The quality of the goalkeeper's visualization speed will be addressed as well. The movements of the striker, as he strikes the ball, serve as a visual cue for the goalkeeper to respond. With consistent training, the goalkeeper's response mechanisms will increase in speed so that responding to a faster, smaller training device will allow him to perform at a higher level.

The initial concept of mini ball training reminds me of a story about former German international star, Franz Beckenbauer. When Franz was a boy in Germany, learning and developing his footballing skills, he used to train with a tennis ball. Franz mastered dribbling, juggling and other foot skills with the tennis ball. He returned to a regulation size ball, he found it much easier to control. The same concept applies to the SPGS training method of using the mini balls or even the SPGS Keeper Ball (weighted medicine ball). When you incorporate a smaller or heavier ball into your weekly training regime, your regulation size ball will seem easier to handle.

When training goalkeepers, you may incorporate the mini ball into a number of shot handling and/or deflecting exercises. As coaches we need to be creative in our exercises, constantly changing the starting position or angle of the goalkeeper. At SPGS, Directors and staff coaches train the goalkeepers using the mini balls by striking balls from the top of the box as well as taking near and far post shots from angles. When using the mini balls to train the goalkeeper's deflecting techniques, it forces the goalkeeper to concentrate on striking the center of the mini ball, which has smaller surface area than a regulation ball. Just like the SPGS Keeper Ball, the mini ball training will expose a weakness in a goalkeeper's saving technique if he cannot read the flight of the ball correctly or make solid contact when deflecting.

The use of mini balls is just one of many innovative training methods which can maximize your goalkeepers' mental capacity while expanding their physical limitations.

"

The way a team plays as a whole determines its success. You may have the greatest bunch of individual stars in the world, but if they don't play together, the club won't be worth a dime.

Babe Ruth

"

RECOGNIZING INJURIES

No athlete wants an injury; no one even expects it. However, injuries occur. By learning the four steps of recognizing and treating injuries, you can most rapidly and completely return to goalkeeping.

The first is the most important. Everyone must be able to "listen" to his body, and know its requirements. When your body requires sleep, food, relaxation or more training - you supply it. So if your play is truly limited due to an injury, it is your responsibility to see that proper care is received.

The second is RICE (Rest, Ice, Compression, Elevation). A general rule for immediate care is to provide RICE for an injury. This prevents pain, as well as lessens the swelling your body will have to get rid of later.

Rest the injury. Get out of the line of fire, even for a short period of time. Many injuries get worse if played on. If the injury turns out to be mild, you can always return as quickly as you stopped.

Ice the injury. An ice bag in a wet towel is a very effective method of numbing the pain, as well as reducing swelling. The area under the ice should get cold and pink. Apply ice for 20-30 minutes. Chemical cold packs stay cold only for 10 minutes; that's not enough time to work effectively.

Compress the injury. A snug (but not tight) elastic bandage will prevent further swelling.

Elevate the injury. Elevating the limb above the level of the heart also minimizes swelling.

The third step is to listen to your physician, athletic trainer or physical therapist when he or she tells you to treat an injury a certain way. Don't aggravate it (and them!) by returning before you are ready.

The fourth step is when injured, work on an aspect of your game you may not have much time for if you weren't hurt. Get involved with your coach and learn field strategy; strengthen another part of your body, or work to build mental strength and discipline. All of these will make you a better athlete and keeper.

Injury Classification
Acute injury occurs when bones, joints, tendons, ligaments or skin are subjected to a strong, abrupt force and the basic structure of the body part is damaged. Fractures, sprains, strains and dislocations of joints are all examples of acute injuries.

Chronic injury, also known as overuse injury results when repeated movements wear down a joint, tendon or ligament causing pain. Tennis elbow or sore knees are examples of chronic injuries.

Major injuries can easily lead to serious disability or to a life or limb-threatening situation. Major injuries include: Head injury or wound, spinal cord or neck injury, unconsciousness, trauma to airway, face injuries, joint trauma or dislocation, breaks or fractures, major lacerations, heatstroke or heat exhaustion, muscle pulls.

Minor injuries are mostly an irritating inconvenience, but they do need to be treated promptly and properly. They include: blisters, bruises, sunburn, cramp, and abrasion.

“

If you don't do what's best for your body, you're the one who comes up on the short end.

Julius Erving

The price of success is hard work, dedication to the job at hand, and to the determination that whether we win or lose, we have applied the best of ourselves to the task at hand.

Vince Lombardi

People say I'm still around because I have a lot of heart, but I know all the heart in the world couldn't have helped me if I wasn't physically fit.

Jimmy Connors

”

PSYCHOLOGICAL

GOOD GOALKEEPING COMES DOWN TO MENTAL SKILLS

After all is said and done,
Good Goalkeeping Still comes down to Mental Skills

In the recent Men's World Cup in France. The names of the best goalkeepers being circulated around were Schmeichel, Van der Sar, Seaman and Keller. These four goalkeepers had solid World Cups and helped their team in varying degrees, but the goalkeepers that stole the show, in my opinion, were Barthez of France and Chilavert of Columbia.

Barthez, even with most of the world waiting for him to make the crucial mistake, enjoyed himself. He played with a confidence that came across as intensity, but not tension. His confidence and outward enjoyment of everything that was happening around him spilled over onto his teammates. In fact, Barthez became the center of pre game rituals like kissing his shaved head. His point blank save against Ronaldo in the final was a perfect indication that he was mentally centered enough to make the big play with the game on the line.

Chilavert also had an outstanding World Cup and carried his team almost to the quarterfinals and beyond with wonderful mental skills. His number one mental skill was his leadership. Incredible leadership, positive yet commanding leadership that continually lifted his team to play beyond themselves. I had the opportunity to watch him play two games during the Kirin Cup in Japan (the USA Women played preliminary games vs the Japanese Women's Nation Team). I was so impressed with his presence in goal, his foot skills and most of all his leadership.

When the "Golden Goal" was scored by Blanc of France thus eliminating Paraquay, it was Chilavert who was picking up his fallen teammates, urging them to pick up their heads and leave the field proudly.

Now, don't get me wrong. To play international soccer and specifically international goalkeeper at the World Cup, you can rest assured all these keepers have pretty solid mental skills. The two I chose just displayed an exceptional level of the "mental package" that was key to their team's success.

So what are the skills that make up the "mental package"?

First, confidence. A keeper must believe in her or himself. This confidence is based on your preparation on the field but also off the field. Every thought you have as an athlete preparing for competition will be a useful thought (will help you play better) or be a destructive thought (will undermine your training). One thing you can be sure of is these thoughts will not just hang out there in limbo.

They will either go into the "help me play better box" or they will go into the "hurt my play box". You can, with mental skills, determine which box those thoughts go into. It has to do with some self talk. How do you see yourself?

In my experience, the best way to impact confidence is to train hard. I always felt as a player when I trained well, I earned the right to play well and that gave me a lot of confidence.

Second, the willingness to compete. The best keepers and athletes take on the challenge of a difficult match. They are willing and ready to compete. They are not thinking about all the pit falls or possible blunders. They are focused on how well they can play, how they can make a difference for their team and how they will be able to deal with any challenge that the other team may create.

This is the proactive, aggressive way to go into a game. If a player goes into a game to try to see what the other team or player brings to the game, they are giving away that edge gained by the player who is ready and willing, who chooses to compete.

Third, leadership. The goalkeepers of the World Cup in France were different types of leaders, but the model leader was, without question, Chilavert. He was demanding, but not degrading. Sometimes I am disappointed when I see keepers yelling and belittling their teammates during the game. Chilavert had the ability to command, even demand, but did so through a positive framework.

Leadership also means taking on the responsibility of organizing the team defensively during an opponent's attack. The best leaders create an atmosphere in which the defenders want to play for you, the goalkeeper, as well as for the team. Chilavert had it and it was an excellent example of leadership at it's very best.

Fourth, composure. One of the pit falls of goalkeeping is when goalkeepers get all caught up in the excitement of the game. They are allowing their emotions to raise to levels in which relaxed muscular function may be impaired and suddenly a shot that seems very savable somehow ends up as a goal scored.

During the Goodwill Games, our first opponent Denmark broke behind our defense down the right flank. Their player was in a position to cross the ball, but instead took a dangerous shot. Briana Scurry shuffled quickly to her left and parried the ball away from the top corner and out of danger for a corner kick. The best part of the play was what happened next, the camera zeroed in on Bri and she was the picture of absolute composure. No big deal, she just made a good save and her body language came across as if it was the most routine play she ever made. This composure is contagious. Her teammates are relaxed, no big deal, we have everything under control and the opponents are thinking wow, that shot didn't even seem to phase her, we'll have to be perfect to score today.

Fifth, concentration. Every keeper who plays at the top levels has this ability. The nature of goalkeeping is inactivity for long stretches of a game and then the keeper has to make a split second decision and often a very athletic response to keep the ball out of the net. This is usually followed by another period of inactivity. Concentration is effected by many variables. One is burn out or just too many games played in a season. Then, the mind starts to wander and that sharp focus isn't as consistent or as easy to achieve. The best keepers monitor this by keeping an even keel body language and demeanor. They never look bored or disinterested, but they seldom are over-active either. They are calm, attentive and mentally centered, waiting patiently for their time to solve a breakdown and shine.

The USA Women's keepers Bri and Tracy Ducar work on concentration during training sessions. Our training sessions are 90 minutes long. The same length of a match. Their objective is to stay sharp, focused and concentrating for those 90 minutes. Even in a game in which they are inactive, they are continually changing their position, communicating to teammates and keeping themselves in the game.

A goalkeeper who gives up soft goals usually suffers from lapses of concentration. The keeper who makes a big play even when his or her team is dominating shows top level mental skills. There may be other mental skills that make up the "mental package". Write and let me know which other skills you feel are important to success at the top levels.

❝

The mind is the limit. As long as the mind can envision the fact that you can do something, you can do it – as long you really believe 100%.
Arnold Schwarzenegger

I remember when I was in college; people told me I couldn't play in the NBA. There's always people saying you can't do it, and those people have to be ignored.
Bill Cartwright, NBA World Champion, Chicago Bulls

THE GOALKEEPER AS THE LEADER

The goalkeeper's responsibility is to prevent goals. No secrets here, but over-looked often, because of their uniqueness within the game of soccer is their role within the team.

The goalkeeper's role within the team is not necessarily different from any other member of the team, but because of his position on the field, he can direct, organize and lead. The keeper must also contribute to chemistry and a strong team when not in the game.

There are two types of leaders:
1. The spiritual leader
2. The tactical leader

Let's first look at the **spiritual leade**r. Often a goalkeeper is the cheerleader from the back of the defense, the spirit within the team. That is fine during practice to keep the level of training up and cheer your teammates on, but during the game, communication should be contained to the task at hand. Does this mean that the goalkeeper shouldn't congratulate a teammate after a good tackle or clear? Absolutely not! Part of being a leader from the keeper position is the ability to get your defenders to play for you. When defenders make a mistake, the best goalkeepers don't jump on their case, they lift them and try to get them back on track so that they can make the next play when it happens. This type of leader provides the juice and is so important to any team because players respond to them. Some **spiritual leaders** are not big talkers but they let their actions speak for them. Little things like 15 minutes extra training before and after practice, or simply giving 100% every time they step on the field for practice and games. Leadership by example is

imperative in developing credibility.

The **tactical leader** is also very important. Some keepers are the eyes for the team, they have the ability to sort out the attack and see who the dangerous players are. They have the ability to organize with little effort and seem to always be one step ahead of the attack. In essence they become coaches on the field.

Both of these descriptions of keepers are descriptions of leaders. Often, the **spiritual leadership** and the **tactical leadership** come from different sources within the team. If, as a goalkeeper, you are neither, then you must reevaluate your role within the team. You are not fulfilling all of your responsibilities to the team.

The world only produces a certain number of Michael Jordan personalities. These players are born leaders. They captivate their audience and inspire their colleagues to perform great feats. As a player it is important to recognize what your personality is and not try to be someone who you are not. That is not to say that you cannot improve your leadership skills. Let's look at the two types of leaders mentioned above and see what you can do to improve in those areas.

The **spiritual leader** is one who is respected by his peers. The quickest way to earn your teammates respect is to train hard and be good at what you do. Players respect talent. If you train hard and improve your skills your teammates will notice. Ask your coach if you can help in the warm up. Maybe the goalkeeper determines what stretches the team does in warm ups. The **spiritual leader** should be positive. Everyone on the team knows when a player makes a mistake and the easiest reaction is to criticize. The spiritual leader will take the time to know his teammates and determine what type of feedback they need. Some players will respond well to a verbal assault but most players would prefer some positive reassurance. Remember that leadership is not merely a popularity contest. It is an ingredient to team success. No-one really believes that Michael Jordan is best buddies with Dennis Rodman.

The **tactical leader** possesses different skills. He has the ability to understand the game and communicate effectively with his teammates. These skills are easier to work on. Many players can spend a career on the field without ever really understanding how the game is played. Playing and coaching are entirely different. As a goalkeeper you should take the time to learn more about the other positions on the field and know what their responsibilities are. If you tell the sweeper to jump in and tackle when he is the last person back you will lose credibility with your sweeper and your coach. The lesson here is to make sure you know what you are talking about. Pay attention during practices and in pre-game talks when the coach is talking to other players. If the opportunity presents itself, watch future opponents play so you can identify tendencies and threats in their attack. You may also want to assist in coaching a younger team to help in your understanding of the game.

The influence of goalkeeper leadership in the game has never been stronger than it is today. In the United States, both Bruce Arena and myself are former US International team goalkeepers. Walter Zenga was the first player/coach in the

MLS in 1999 with the New England Revolution. Italy recently appointed former National team goalkeeper Dino Zoff to the position of Head Coach. Zoff captained the Italians to the World Cup in 1982. The 1998 World Cup gave us a cast of goalkeepers who personified leadership, Chilavert (Paraguay) and Schmeichel (Denmark) being the most noticeable.

In the early eighties Bruce Grobbelaar revolutionized goalkeeping in England by consistently coming for and winning crosses 15 yards from his goal. Other goalkeepers took notice and realized that it was no longer sufficient to only win balls in the 6 yard box. English keepers began to extend their range. The introduction of the back pass rule in the early 90's exposed keepers who had poor ball control with their feet. The effect was that goalkeepers had to transform their game to become competent field players as well as good goalkeepers. All goalkeepers should be looking to improve their game to give themselves a competitive edge over the opposition. Whether you are playing in High School, College or MLS you will have to compete against some other goalkeeper for the starting position. As goalkeepers get older the comparative difference in their technical and physical abilities decreases. What separates the best from the rest is their psychological and tactical skills. Today, the better goalkeepers have taken on the responsibility of leadership within their teams. Those who combine quality leadership with good goalkeeping are setting a higher standard for all goalkeepers.

A man has to have goals – for a day, for a lifetime – and that was mine, to have people say, "There goes Ted Williams, the greatest hitter who ever lived."

Ted Williams. Boston Red Sox

We all have dreams. But in order to make dreams into reality, it takes an awful lot of determination, dedication, self-discipline and effort.

Jesse Owens, Olympian

EVERYONE HAS A CHOICE: TO WIN OR LOSE

Most top athletes agree that mental skills are among the best qualities to have when competing. But are mental skills the same as physical ones - a "head" version of diving, catching or kicking? What do we actually mean by "mental skills?" Exactly how do they produce champions?

I define winning not as having the better score at the end of every game, but as "consistently playing to your personal best." Think of the games when you were at your best. In your mind, you knew the other team would have to be pretty darn good - beyond excellent! - to score. Every play seemed to come easily. Think how good you could be if you played like that during every practice and game!

I define losing not as being on the low end of a score, but as "never releasing yourself from your own fears." These can include fear of losing, fear of failure, fear of embarrassment, fear of training. Of course, training can sometimes leave you feeling uncomfortable, exhausted or drained - but that's not losing.

So what qualities produce a winner?

Positive self-expectations.

This means the overall attitude needed to express real enthusiasm and optimism. The body expresses what the mind is concerned about. In other words, a person usually gets what he or she expects. Work on the skills of expecting the best. By doing so, you prepare yourself physically, as well as mentally, for the demands of the goalkeeper position. Ask yourself: Am I generally optimistic? Do I expect the best for myself? How do I respond following a mistake? Do I feel self-pity, or do I look at the problem with the confidence that "I can correct it, and do better next time?" Ask yourself: As a person, how do I accept praise and criticism? For years, every time someone said to me, "Tony great game!" I would make excuses as to why I was lucky, or I'd downplay my own performance. Now I have learned to look that person in the eye and say, "Thank you!"

Learn to use positive self-talk, as the best athletes and goalkeepers do. This means saying to yourself, "I was good today - and I can be even better tomorrow," or "Next time I'll get it - I can do it!" Think about your talents. Pretty impressive, aren't they? Try to review problems as opportunities. Stay relaxed (this skill is vital to every goalkeeper). Be intense - but not tense. Many goalkeepers get caught up in the tension as a game winds down - with the result that they allow a goal that is beneath their level. As anxiety levels rise, the best keepers "hold it together" and relieve themselves of the tension that can inhibit performance.

Positive self-motivation.
Try to focus on rewards and successes, rather than on the fear of conceding a goal. Motivation is an inside job. Try to be motivated with desires. Say to yourself, "I want to do it - and I can do it!"

Ask yourself how you are motivated. Is it by the fear of failure, or the drive and attention to attain the joys of your vision? At times fear can be a great motivator - but too often athletes become obsessed with the penalties of failure. Take an inventory of the type of questions you ask yourself. Do you say, "Why can't I do it?" This type of question leads to the wrong answers - basically, all the reasons why you are failing. Instead, phrase the question differently: "What do I have to do to handle that crossed ball?" Then the right answers will come cascading down! Do this exercise. Write down your visions as a goalkeeper. Add your most important personal desires. Now write down the benefits of achieving them. Keep this list handy, and read it whenever that old self-doubt comes creeping in. Look for role models - people who have achieved what you want, or are current-ly doing what you hope to do. Pick some of their best qualities, and incorporate them into your behavior. Become obsessed with learning - and learn from the best.

Positive self-image.
Imagination is an incredible tool. It can be used not only for entertainment, but to develop and even create one's own self-image. Visualize yourself making a save; now replay it in slow motion. Feel the vision as realistically as possible; fan-tasize the goalkeeper and person you would like to become. Feel yourself grow-ing - achieving - winning!

Everyone, no matter how young or old, should have dreams, and everyone should visualize accomplishing them. Remember: Your imagination rules your world. Set aside 15 minutes each day to relax, meditate and imagine yourself achieving your goals. Picture yourself making great saves and big plays. Make those images as vivid as possible. Smell the field; feel the sensation of the crowd; sense the fantastic feeling as you hit the ground after a great diving save.

Here's one more exercise. Read a newspaper or magazine article about a keeper who had a great game. Now picture yourself making all the same plays.

Positive self-direction.

So now you know where you want to go; it's time for a plan of action to make it happen. If you never define your goals, or never create a plan to accomplish them, then you'll never realize your goals. This happens to so many talented keepers.

Sense what is needed, and trust that you can achieve it. Where do you want to be in three years? One year? What's your most important priority this month? Create a calendar and a journal that enables you to plot out what you need to accomplish. This gives you a timetable to see what you are learning and how you are growing as a person along the way.

Positive self-control

You must accept full responsibility for yourself. You have the power to control your life; now assume the responsibility for it. Take credit for where you are as a goalkeeper; you've already accomplished a lot. But remember! You are in the driver's seat. You can still learn how to respond and adapt more quickly to the demands of your position by accepting the responsibility of creating your own breaks and gains.

Understand that setbacks, when they occur, are not fun or wished for, but they can provide direction and motivation. No successful person has ever gone through life without some setbacks or failures. Take the credit for your successes but also accept the blame when it is appropriate. Don't wait for an invitation to succeed. Write your own ticket to where you want to be, and then go for it. List the habits you want to change and list what you want to exchange them for. Renew your dedication for the next 30 days and then see how far you have come.

Try this final exercise. Look in the mirror. What do you see? What you see is really your choice, just as is your choice to win or lose.

TEN STEPS TO A WINNING EDGE

Tal Fletcher, parent of Soccer Plus Goalkeeper School student Tal Jr, presented the following thoughts to Tony DiCicco.

1. Are you coachable? Can you take criticism without looking for an alibi? Are you a know-it-all? Do you always try to improve?

2. Are you a positive team member? Do you contribute to team morale, or do you bellyache and complain? Are you up when things go your way, down when they don't? Do you support your teammates and coaches, or do you knock them?

3. Are you possessed with the spirit of competition which fires an intense desire to be successful? Do you never take "no" for an answer when there's a job to be done? Does it bother you to give less than 100%?

4. Are you mentally tough? When the going gets tough, do you get tougher? Does the screaming crowd or crucial situation shake you up - or make you rise to the challenge? Do you make excuses, or do you suck it up and get the job done?

5. How are you under pressure? Can you concentrate on what must be done? Can you shut out of your mind a previous failure, foul or personal insult in order to give special attention to the play that is happening here and now?

6. Do you have an ardent desire to improve? Are you eager to work diligently on your skills, especially those you are weak in?

7. Are you willing to practice? Do you just put in your time, or do you practice with the same intensity you bring to a match?

8. Are you willing to make sacrifices?

9. Are you willing to be impersonal toward your opponent? Do you shut out such feelings as fear and anger, except to play as hard as possible within the rules?

10. Are you willing to fulfill your responsibility as an athlete? Do you recognize that your attitude and actions - on and off the field - must be those of a class person representing a class program?

TALKING TO YOURSELF

Be careful what you say.

An athlete talking to themselves during competition is hardly a new phenomenon. Tennis player John McEnroe was infamous for his outbursts on the court at umpires and himself. Trash talking has become more and more popular in recent years. Many people believe that this type of talk is as much to motivate the talker, as it is to disparage the opponent. The talk does not have to be vocal. By merely thinking you are talking to yourself and sending a message. Self-talk is any message that you send to yourself.

The messages that you send to yourself have a direct impact on your performance. Your thoughts influence what you are feeling. How you are feeling affects your self-esteem. If you have a high level of self-esteem you are more likely to perform at your highest level. With that in mind athletes need to learn to listen to their self talk and recognize what type of message they are sending.

Self-talk comes in two major forms. The first is general and the second is specific. An example of general talk would be a goalkeeper telling himself something like this before a game. "You have worked hard to make yourself a very good goalkeeper. You have put the time in on the training field and you are prepared to play. Good things happen to players who train hard". This is an example of a goalkeeper affirming his confidence in himself to play well. An example of specific talk might occur on a breakaway when the goalkeeper sees the forward coming through. "Stay on your toes, don't commit until the forward takes a long touch." Specific talk often incorporates cue words. These words set off a predetermined stream of thoughts. Look at the breakaway again. The goalkeeper may use "patience" as a cue word. By merely saying that one word the brain translates the message into " Don't rush out. Stand up as long as you can. Wait for the forward to take a long touch". Specific talk can also happen in the pregame when the goalkeeper mentally rehearses situations that he feels will occur during the game.

The examples listed above are all positive statements that the goalkeeper has made to himself. The reality is that we all say negative things to ourselves as well. You go to the game, get dressed to play, pull out your gloves and realize you forgot to wash them. The initial reaction will probably be annoyance at yourself for forgetting. You are not annoyed that you forgot, you are annoyed that you have to play a game with dirty gloves and you may not be able to catch the ball very well. At this point you need to recognize that the message you are sending is an excuse for not playing well in the upcoming game. Now it is time to send a positive message. "I will dampen the gloves with some water now to improve the grip. I have played well with dirty gloves at practice before and I will play well again today. I have very good catching technique that will help. Imagine if I had forgotten to bring my gloves altogether. It's OK. I'm going to play well today." Negative self-talk is quick to appear after a mistake in a game; a dropped cross, a shanked punt, a failure to communicate with your defense. One mistake does not make you a bad goalkeeper. Instead of saying "I'm horrible at crosses. I hope they don't send over any more" try this: "I've caught hundreds of crosses in games before. I hope they send over another so that I can win it and start a counter attack." The trick here is recognizing when the negative self talk begins and reversing the trend quickly. Negative talk quickly becomes a self-fulfilling prophecy. The ability to recognize the switch from positive to negative is an acquired skill. As your emotions are caught up in the game you need to monitor the thoughts and talk in your head.

While positive talk is important it must be realistic. We are all capable of over-achieving but the possibilities are not endless. Therefore we must primarily focus on playing up to our potential. Be honest with yourself and put an emphasis on your strengths when you motivate yourself. Remember whom you are talking to. You know your body and your abilities better than anyone else. Our biggest disappointments come when we do not perform the tasks that we know we can on a consistent basis. Incredible saves are a bonus, but goalkeepers are judged by their ability to make the saves that they are supposed to make.

Careful monitoring of the messages you send to yourself will result in a constant stream of positive messages and an increase in your levels of self-esteem and confidence. To achieve peak physical performance you will need peak mental performance.

Setting goals for your game is an art. The trick is in setting them at the right level. Never too high and never too low. A good goal should be lofty enough to inspire hard work, yet realistic enough to provide solid hope of attainment.

Greg Norman, Golfer

I always felt that my greatest asset was not my physical ability, but my mental ability.

Bruce Jenner

COMMUNICATION

It is possible to play a complete game in goal without touching the ball and still have a great game. One of the goalkeeper's responsibilities is to organize the team defensively during the course of the game. If this is done effectively the opposing offense can be stopped from penetrating the defense and getting any scoring opportunities.

The simplest form of communication is for the goalkeeper to call "keeper" when he wants the ball. This in itself is very helpful but it is only the tip of the iceberg. For a goalkeeper to communicate at the highest level he must have a very good understanding of the game. Here are some things he should be able to recognize and understand.

1. Tendencies of strikers.
2. Systems of play.
3. Defensive principles.
4. Defensive mismatches.
5. Strengths and weaknesses of your teammates.
6. Responsibilities of defenders.

In essence the goalkeeper needs to be a coach of sorts in the goal. Once the goalkeeper has that knowledge he must figure out how he can apply it to the benefit of the team. When instructing your team it is not always necessary to use complete sentences. In fact, one word will often suffice. For example if the ball is loose in the box and the keeper wants a defender to quickly kick the ball upfield to safety the word "CLEAR" should get the message across. Other one word examples could be "CONTAIN," "TIME," "OUT," or "MAN-ON." Often there is not enough time for more than a one-word instruction.

The tone of voice is also important. As a keeper you want to appear to be calm, poised and in control. Your speech should be authoritative, clear and confident. If your teammates sense panic in your voice they will lose confidence in you. If your voice is too passive they may not process your message immediately and certainly will not act with any sense of urgency. Experience alone will dictate to you what tone of voice works best. Your tone will also differ when talking to your defense after a play. In time you learn which style works best with each individual defender. For example, if you criticize defender "A" aggressively for letting a forward turn in the box it might be the kick in the rear they needed not to let it happen again.

Defender "B" may be insulted or embarrassed by the same approach and end up sulking for the rest of the game. Each defender has his own personality and the goalkeeper needs to know which approach will work best.

Whereas communication is obviously a good thing, too much of a good thing is bad. If you talk continuously throughout the game your own players will tune you out. They will hear you but they are no longer listening to you. Therefore you should only give instructions when it is important.

One way of making sure a defender hears you is by using his name. This works for three reasons. 1) Most people like to be called by their name 2) The sound of your own name immediately attracts your attention and 3) If the keeper says "John, get tight to #9" then John knows that everybody else knows that he should be tighter to #9. It's basic accountability.

As with all aspects of team play you must practice first. Everybody on the team must know exactly what each instruction means. Different teams use different words. To close a forward down who is threatening to shoot, a goalkeeper may shout "CLOSE," "PRESSURE," or "STEP." It really doesn't matter what you say as long as the player knows what you mean. These issues should be sorted out with your coach and team on the practice field.

The number of scoring opportunities presented to opponents is greatly affected by the goalkeeper's ability to communicate. Good communication may not improve your save percentage but it will improve your goals against.

COMMUNICATION AND TEAM SHAPE

To be a good goalkeeper you must possess many skills. Most keepers start off in goal because they are good shot stoppers or because they have good hands. The more they play in goal they develop their technical and tactical skills. They recognize threats to the goal and deal with them effectively. The highest level of the position is preventative goalkeeping skills. These are often difficult to see and there are no stats kept except for the most important, Goals Against.

Preventative goalkeeping skills deprive the opposition of quality scoring opportunities. The most effective way to do this is to prevent the opposition from possessing the ball in your final third. Obviously as a goalkeeper you are physically limited by the confines of the goal so you must verbally direct your teammates to perform the tasks at hand. There are five steps to improve your preventative goalkeeping skills.

#1 Know the Game

Young goalkeepers should become students of the game of soccer in addition to being players. Check with your local state association and see when you can take your USSF "E" or "F" coaching license. You could also volunteer to be an assistant coach of a younger team. These experiences will offer you a different perspective on the game and help you understand the roles of individual players and their responsibilities on the field.

#2 Know Your System of Play

What style of defense does your team play? Do you have a sweeper or do you play flat at the back? Do you play man to man or do you play zonal? At what place on the field does your team start to pressure the ball? Do your outside midfielders force attackers inside or outside? Do you use an offside trap? Where is your restraining line to defend set pieces from 50 yards, 35 yards? How does your team defend corner kicks and long throw ins?

These are all basic tactical decisions that your coach has decided upon and your team should play accordingly. However, theory and practice are different and players will have to be reminded constantly throughout the game. If you do not know what is supposed to be going on you cannot properly direct your teammates.

#3 Know Your Teammates

No two players are alike. Your two outside full backs will probably have the same responsibilities but they will not play alike. Learn their strengths and weaknesses. One defender may be particularly fast and therefore not have to mark his man very tightly because he can recover quickly. However, if he leaves too big a gap he may not be able to catch up. If you think the gap is too big let him know. Your other defender may not be as fast and prefer to mark tightly. But there may be times in the game when he will need to drop off a little and provide some depth. Know which midfielders are good at tackling. Those who are not should be encouraged to delay the player on the ball until there is adequate cover. You should not ask your teammates to do something that they are unable to do. One player may be able to switch the point of attack by driving the ball from one side of the field to the other, whereas another player may not have the strength to do so. The more you know about your teammates the better information you will be able to provide.

#4 Recognize and Correct Problems

This is where your improved knowledge of the game will become an advantage. Most people can look at the replay of a goal and tell you where the breakdown occurred that led to the goal. They are as helpful as Monday morning quarterbacks. You can really help your team by recognizing problems as they are happening, do something to avert the danger and then make the adjustments so that it doesn't happen again. You may think that's the coach's job and it is. However, players on the field can often spot problems first and no-one is in a better position to do so than the goalkeeper. Recognizing the problem is difficult but correcting it can often be harder. In these circumstances some advanced thinking can help. In the days prior to a game try to anticipate some of the things that could go wrong. If your team is playing with an offside trap but the opposition is getting in behind your defense do you abandon the trap or look to see why it is not working as well as it did in your other games. Maybe your midfield is not putting pressure on the ball. That can be corrected. Maybe one of your defenders is slow stepping up. That can be corrected. Maybe the referee's assistant is having a bad day. Abandon the trap.

The key here is to prepare yourself for as many contingencies as possible. This is one of the reasons why professional goalkeepers are older than most of their teammates. The more experience you have the easier it is to identify and correct problems. They may not be as strong and as quick as their younger counterparts but their anticipation and on field coaching make up for any physical deficiencies.

#5 Post Game Evaluation

Not every issue can be corrected in the game. When a game is over you should take a little time to reflect on how you played and how the team performed. Jot down any issues that need to be addressed and discuss them with your coach so that you can correct them as a team on the practice field. Caution! Always remember that thinking like a coach does not make you the coach. You may disagree with your coach on some issues and that's O.K. as long as you make your points in a constructive manner and accept the coach's decision as final at the end of any tactical discussion.

The amount of communication required will depend upon the ability level of your teammates and your system of play. In the traditional sweeper system you will talk mostly to the sweeper and he will direct the defense from his position. In a flat back 3 or 4 the goalkeeper is required to communicate a lot more directly with all his defenders. A man to man defense is fairly simplistic in that every player knows his role and it is easy to see if a player is not doing his job. A zonal defense is a lot more complicated and the goalkeeper must help out his defenders as forwards are passed on from zone to zone. You may also find that one of your central defenders is the team captain and he is very vocal. If someone else on the team is giving the same instructions that you are thinking there is no need to repeat the message.

As you can see, the art of communication is simple in principal but complex in execution. The keeper must have the confidence to direct his defense and the knowledge to give the right information. He must also know what tone of voice to use with different players and when to talk and when to be quiet. The goal of any goalkeeper is not to concede any goals. There will always be an incredible amount of satisfaction by shutting out a team and making 6 or 7 brilliant saves but you will learn to equally enjoy the pleasure of shutting out a team by shutting down their offense with solid preventative goalkeeping skills.

"

The world is filled with willing people, some willing to work, some willing to let them.
Robert Frost

The fight is won or lost far away from the witnesses. It is won behind the lines, in the gym and out there on the road, long before I dance under those lights.
Muhammad Ali

NON-VERBAL GOALKEEPER COMMUNICATION

We all know how important communication is by the goalkeeper. The ability to organize the defensive team in itself saves goals. It saves goals because there are fewer opportunities, less shots and less confidence by the attacking opponent that they can break down the defense.

When we think of communication, we think of verbal commands coming from the goalkeeper that are concise, specific and in a tone of voice that is confident and reflects the need or lack of need for urgency. However, not all communication is verbal, in fact, some of the most important communication coming from the keeper position may be body language, pointing, posture etc. So what are some of these non-verbal communication skills necessary for keepers to have?

First for sure is the communication to teammates and opponents that the keeper can handle whatever comes his or her way. It's a presence that some keepers have and it comes from doing all the simple things very.....well, simply. Like handling a backpass and not making it an adventure or having a cross sent over and winning it without some of the dramatics that some keepers add to their game. You've seen them, the twisting crashing to the ground catch, when a simple "high contour" controlled snag is all that was needed. When the simple things are done easily, the message to the opponent is that we have to do something much more difficult to break down this keeper. So maybe they try to over-whip their crosses into the box and instead of hitting it perfectly, they miss it and the effect of the attack is lost. What about the message to teammates? If the keeper communicates that everything is under control by each easy play they make, the defenders feel free to join into the attack instead of over-compensating defensively. You always hear about two keepers on a team and one seems to always get an extra goal to work with from his team and the other keeper always has to win games 1-0 etc. Sometimes this is due to keeper #1 communicating an "everything is under control" message and teammates are released to attack and take control of the game more.

Non-verbal communication isn't only important when things are going well. The best keepers even under siege by the opponent have a way of giving confidence to their teammates. I think Briana Scurry of the USA Women's National Team and Olympic Gold Medal winners has this communication skill. When we were playing Sweden in the second game of the Olympics, we had a 2-1 lead late in the game. The Swedes knew they were eliminated if they lost, so they threw everything they had forward. The game could have gotten a bit out of control, but Briana always seem to come for the ball just when we needed her to and a promising Swedish attack ended up in our keeper's secure hands. I have seen so many games end up in a panic with the keeper most panicked and the team following right behind. What's your communication like when the game is on the line and it's a bit frantic and you and your team are trying to hold onto a one-goal lead? Do you instill confidence and control to your team or is your communication sending the message of Custer's last stand? I can tell you first hand that the best keepers seem to get calmer as the game gets more scrappy and frantic. There are other non-verbal messages and communication that keeper's can give for more tactical purposes. Take the keeper that just wins a through ball or a cross and now with body language, looks up and long, towards the strikers and is saying, "let's try a counterattack on this long drop kick, so get on the end of it."

In a backpass situation when a defender is chasing a ball towards his or her own goal, the goalkeeper can and should give verbal commands, but it's also a big help to the defender if there is a non-verbal command like pointing towards the touch-line if you want the ball taken or kicked outside.

Another tactical situation that could use a non-verbal command is when the attack is coming down one flank, if the keeper can find a teammate and shout and point towards the far post, the words take on a dimension of urgency and that player will get back and cover that back post. In summary, just remember, you are always sending signals and messages. Your teammates and opponents read them and some of these messages create positive results and some don't.

A ship in the harbor is safe, but that's not what ships are built for.
Anonymous

Shilton looks back:
A lot's happened down the years. It's a long time since I hung on the banister of my parents stairs, sandbags tied to my ankles, trying to grow tall enough to be a goalkeeper.

MENTAL IMAGERY

The difference between a good goalkeeper and a great one lies in mental conditioning. With most keepers, correct technique eventually becomes automatic; at some point the mental side of the game became more important than the physical aspect. Bill Steffen, SPGS Director and Head Coach at University of Oregon, talked to SoccerPlus Goalkeeper School students about the mental side of goalkeeping.

"Here's an imagery exercise," Bill began. "Sit with your hands straight at your sides; put your feet on the floor. Close your eyes. Take a deep breath; let it out slowly. See yourself on the field. A cross comes from the left; you move to your right and catch it"

There are two types of mental imagery: **external and internal**. In the above example external imagery would be used by a keeper who looked at him or herself as if on a TV screen, and watched the save as it occurred. That's valuable for a nervous keeper; he or she can watch the save being made, gaining confidence that way.

Internal imagery, on the other hand, is used to solve problems with your body. A keeper using internal imagery would break the save down step by step, actually feeling each part of the play as it "happened."

Why should keepers use imagery? Quite simply, to become better athletes. Bill explained: "Relax. Picture a field, with you in goal. See the grass, the sky; see the cross coming from left to right. Field it cleanly. Now, rewind the 'tape' to before the cross. This time as it comes, concentrate only on your feet. Shuffle, push off, catch the ball. Now rewind it again, and concentrate only on your legs. Pump with short, quick steps; power up to jump and catch. Rewind the tape another time; now feel your shoulders and arms. Pump across the goalmouth; reach up and catch the ball. Rewind the tape one more time. Concentrate this time on your hands; make a fist, drop, push up, and feel the ball snugly hit your hands. And rewind it again. Now just see the ball coming from left to right; see it as it stops in your hands. Now open your eyes.

The reason for breaking down this mental daydream, Bill said, is to "concentrate on the important things - footwork, positioning, jumping - to try to reinforce them in your mind, so you can eventually do them correctly, often. Why can't you always perform the collapse dive correctly? You know what it feels like - but you can't always duplicate it. That's where imagery helps. It's a way of practicing without even taking the field."

When should you use imagery? "All the time," Bill said simply. "Use it at night before a game if you're nervous; during 'down time'; when you're driving to a game (but don't close your eyes when you're driving!); before a game, instead of thinking about previous mistakes."

The payoffs from imagery may not be immediate, Bill warned - "But you'll play better down the line. I won't know if you never use imagery, and neither will your coach - but you will. Believe me, it works."

Another important area of mental skills Bill discussed involved goals (no, not the ones you defend, these are things you hope to achieve).

There are two kinds of goals, he said: performance goals and outcome goals. An outcome goal - say, winning a match, getting a shutout, even making a team - are based on areas over which you may have little or no control (your teammates, coach or a referee can determine who wins a match or gets a shutout; someone you've never met may determine whether or not you make a team).

However, you yourself determine performance goals. A good performance goal could be working on punting four times a week, or practicing weak-side diving every other day.

"If you focus too much on outcome goals you'll be disappointed," Bill said. "But performance goals - that's where you really measure progress, and improve."

It's important to set a time frame or structure for your goals, he added. When he lived in New York he ran the stairs of the Empire State Building. All 86 flights! That's pretty daunting, so Bill focused first on 10 flights at a time. At 70 he'd get winded, so he set his goals on five at a time. Gradually, by the time he hit the top, he'd focus on just one step at a time.

"It sounds silly, but those were all realistic goals," Bill said. "I was able to adapt my goals as necessary."

Similarly, he said, while setting a goal of "making the national team" is admirable, it's too far in the future. "Set a more realistic goal, in a more realistic time frame. Maybe it's making the state or regional team, or just learning more about what it takes to be a national team player."

Sometimes, of course, outsiders - parents, coaches, teammates - set goals for you, and those goals may be unrealistic. The best thing to do then, Bill said, is to sit down with those people, discuss your goals and what they expect of you, and together come up with reasonable things to accomplish.

Winning is not an all time thing. You don't win once in a while you don't do things right once in a while, then you do them right all of the time. Winning is habit. Unfortunately, so is losing.

Vince Lombardi

The principle is competing against yourself. It's about self-improvement, about being better than you were the day before.

Steve Young

SELF ESTEEEM

Improve Performance by Improving Self Esteeem

There is a direct correlation between self-esteem and performance. When your self-esteem (your confidence in yourself) is high, your performance is enhanced. Conversely, when your self-esteem is low, your performance suffers. Make sense? It should. Just think of the games you played well; try to remember the feelings you had leading up to them. I guarantee you felt good about yourself, about your preparation, about the upcoming contest and your play reflected that positive attitude.

I've been training goalkeepers with both the men's U-20 and the women's full national team. I trained these keepers to feel good about themselves. My goal was to get them into matches "in the right place mentally." I knew that if they entered a game with a high level of self-esteem, their performance would be solid.

I tried to reinforce the feeling that they had trained hard and well, and earned the right to play well. I also tried to convey the message that many of the plays we keepers must make are fun. Our game is fun - and the plays we make are fun. One of the big problems young goalkeepers must overcome is not physical, technical or tactical. It is the negative and damaging self-talk they say to themselves. Keepers who attempt a play yet come up short invariably are harder on themselves than if a teammate tried a similarly difficult play and failed. They would say to the teammate, "Forget it; you'll do it next time." But they are far less patient with themselves, and pepper their brains with questions like, "Why am I so bad on that play? What's wrong with me?"

There are two problems here. First, such self-talk is not going to help performance. It would have been much better (though more difficult) to say to yourself, "Relax. I know I can make that play. I'll do better next time."

Second, when you ask questions like those above, you receive the wrong type of answers. Picture your brain as a tremendous computer. Whenever you ask it a question, it searches its memory bank for answers. If you ask the wrong question - like "Why am I so bad today?" - it produces answers like "You have trouble with crossed balls" or "You didn't train hard enough!" Those answers don't help at all!

Start to monitor the kind of questions you ask yourself. Make sure your questions are positive and future-directed ("What do I need to do to make that play consistently?") rather than negative and backward-looking ("Why do I always foul up that play?").

Remember: Have fun - and enjoy the competition and the challenges of goalkeeping. They help you grow as a person. Good luck!

How can you improve your self-esteem, and therefore your performance?

Try these simple exercises:
- Write down three things you did each day that you are proud of.
- Set a very obtainable performance goal. For example: "I am going to train every other day this week on footwork."
- Sit with a few teammates. Take turns saying something good about everyone else in the group.
- Each time you doubt yourself - even a little - say: "I belong! I am confident! I am proud!"
- Take 10 minutes each day to sit comfortably in a chair, visualizing a save or play you want to make regularly. Now rewind it on your "mental recorder"; play it forward in slow motion and - as clearly and vividly as you can - visualize it. Repeat this procedure three times.
- Confirm to yourself that playing goalkeeper is fun. It is not without drawbacks of course, but - much more than not - it is a lot of fun!

❝

Do not let what you cannot do interfere with what you can do.
John Wooden

I hated every minute of the training, but I said, "Don't quit. Suffer now and live the rest of your life as a champion.
Muhammad Ali

COLLEGE SOCCER

GOING TO COLLEGE

BY TRACY DUCAR

Tracy Ducar played for National powerhouse UNC Chapel Hill and won three National Championships before joining the US National team. As a former SPGS student she can easily relate to the dilemma facing college bound players. Here Tracy shares some ideas to help with your decision making process.

For some of you the college selection process is over, for others it's buried in the past, for some it's a long way off into the future, but for many it's just around the bend. When I was a camper at the SoccerPlus Goalkeeper School I know I gained a lot of valuable information from the staff that lectured on preparing for college and how to select a college. And although this lecture is still part of the SPGS program, I felt it might be helpful to have some of the major points of the lecture in writing. The following are areas that I found extremely helpful when it was my time to figure out where I wanted to go and what I wanted to accomplish.

Things to consider when choosing a college:
First off, what is the academic reputation of the school and is this consistent with your personal expectations. Basic, but worth mentioning, does the school offer the major of your choice? And how important is population size to you? Are you looking for a large student population or are you more comfortable in a smaller environment. How far from home do you want to be ... do you have responsibilities that require you to be close to home? Would you prefer a setting in a city, suburb, and country? How much do you know about the personalities of your future soccer teammates ... do you sense that you will fit in with them and with the general population that you have been exposed to? If playing is real important to you, do you have an idea of what your playing opportunities are going to be? How many other goalkeepers will you be competing with? And something that is important to ask yourself, would you still be happy with this particular school if you had a career-ending injury and were unable to play soccer?

How to get noticed by a college coach:
Of course, being a standout on your high school and/or club team might spark some attention. Playing for a club team that participates in high profile tournaments (such as WAGS, the Dallas Cup, the San Diego Surf Cup) could prove valuable. Taking part in the Olympic Development Program (ODP) is especially beneficial because college coaches recognize the ODP as a place to view several potential recruits at one site and at one time. You can also take a more personal approach and write to a coach directly and possibly send along a video of your-

self in action in the net ... this is a great way to differentiate yourself from the crowd. And if you send a letter, here is some advice: make the letter personal ... use the school's name and the coach's name - let them know you know who they are and that this is important to you. Be honest ... don't stretch the truth. Include in your letter your upcoming soccer schedule, which would allow them to see you in action. Attach a soccer resume with your address and phone number; GPA; academic scores (SAT or ACT); class rank/class size; academic honors; other clubs, activities, or sports; high school team information (coach's name, number of years on varsity, team record, G.A.A., shutouts, save percentage); club team information; soccer honors; list any camp experience (i.e., SoccerPlus - note whether you took part in the Challenge program or NTC); 3-5 references (names, addresses, phone numbers) - be sure to check with the people you are listing as a reference before you list them - feel confident that they will give you a positive recommendation and consider using a rival coach or a referee ... it would be expected that they would give an unbiased opinion of your play. Be concise ... your resume should not exceed a page in length.

What else?:
You should make a wish list of schools, being realistic about your abilities and talents. Of course, you should apply to more than one school ... possibly apply to a "reach" school and a "safety" school because you never know what will or can happen. Get out to see as many of the school teams as you reasonably can and try to meet as many of the players as possible. Be sure to visit as many schools as is reasonable. And if you can, don't let scholarship amounts heavily sway your decision ... remember few schools give out FULL scholarships these days. Most schools divvy up the dollars between several different players. And most important, try to arrange an individual meeting with the coach.

What should you ask of a coach?: Certainly you may have your own questions, but here are a few suggestions: if you don't already know, ask what the academic entrance requirements are. Find out what the goalkeeper situation is (look for honesty in the coach's answer ... be wary of a coach who does not seem to be telling the truth.) Find out if their team has a separate goalkeeper coach and if so, what is the expertise of this person. Ask about the opportunity to earn a scholarship once on the team ... can this happen? What has happened in the past when a scholarship recipient has been injured ... did they lose their scholarship? What is expected during the off-season? Where are the weight training facilities - ask for a tour of these facilities. Find out if there is an academic center for athletes with counselors and tutors? Again, you will have some of your own personal questions, these are just a few that you might find useful.

What are college coaches looking for in their players: Of course these are just generalizations, but here are a few areas and characteristics that coaches have consistently noted as important: attitude (are you a team player or a self-centered performer); what are your physical/technical abilities/ limitations; do you demonstrate leadership characteristics; how do you handle yourself after being scored upon; do you possess courage, confidence, composure, determination, commitment, intelligence, self-discipline; what is your level of consistency; how do you manage your fitness?

Academic Preparation: Plan to take your SAT's or ACT's in your junior year. If it is possible, take AP and honors classes. Take AP and achievement exams to receive credit for college courses when possible. Strive for the best grades possible (college coaches hesitate to recruit players they fear may not remain academically eligible).

Athletic Preparation: Get fit and stay fit!!!! Have a weight-training program that you follow religiously. Play as often as you can and at the highest level possible. No amount of training can replace game experience.

WHAT A COLLEGE LOOKS FOR IN A PLAYER

BY ANSON DORRANCE

The way I answer the question is by telling the story about a Supreme Court judge in Southern California who was asked to define pornography. He had to write a statute and he took twelve months trying to sort out an appropriate definition of pornography. After a whole year, this very intelligent man could not write the statute. So they asked him, "How do you know what pornography is?" He said, "I know it when I see it."

It's basically the same with players. I can tell you a player needs certain technical, tactical, physical and psychological levels, and yet I can find a player who has won either a world championship or gold medal who doesn't have a dimension that I'm saying you require. What you need is some kind of balance. But rest assured, it is critical to be extraordinary in at least one area. Then you will have an impact. If you can out-head everybody in the world but can trap a ball farther than you can kick it, you can have an impact. If you are a psychological rock, but have no tactical awareness, you can have an impact.

The great players, obviously, are extraordinary in more than one area, and the greatest players are extraordinary in all areas. It's based on a mix of all these different qualities. I would say the most important of all these qualities is your psychological strength, because the quality that separates winners is the ability constantly to reach down to find something deep inside them to make the commitment other people are not willing to make. With that in mind, here are the four dimensions that I believe are necessary.

Psychological

This is the capacity to be able to deal with all kinds of adversity. It is also the capacity to be so hard that in your duels with opposing players you are not intimidated. In great duels there are defining moments. There is the moment when you get a sense of the other person's hardness. It may be a physical risk issue or a fitness issue.

When you are competing, you measure your capacity to take physical risks, your capacity to push through pain threshold, and your capacity not to back down psychologically from someone. Those defining moments are constant in contact sports. If two players are running for the same ball, the one with the weaker psychological dimension is going to time it so she gets to the ball late. In other words, she is going to time it so she misses the confrontation with the other player. That's the defining moment of the duel - who is going to slow down and who isn't.

Physical

A lot of this is inherited - your quickness, your speed, your agility and your strength. But some of it can be developed. You can improve your quickness, your endurance and, to a certain extent, you can develop speed. The person who fills the physical dimension is the one who has an intelligent and consistent work ethic to improve all the physical qualities. The reason I say "intelligent" is that most people don't have the understanding that all these things work against each other. For instance, the process of developing speed actually retards agility. If you are developing a good cardiovascular base, it actually hurts your speed development. If you are running 20 or 30 minutes over miles and miles, it actually detracts from your ability to sprint. You need to develop a balance of these qualities.

Technical

Speed of play is the critical element in a player's tactical development. Speed of play is your ability to do things quickly with a soccer ball. A four-year-old can trap a ball. But does this mean this player can trap a ball? Actually, no. This four-year-old can't trap a ball on a full run when another player is trying to cut him/her off at the kneecaps.

As you go from one level to the next technically, you are required to be able to do things so much faster - shoot under pressure, do things with the ball without time and space, and do things with one touch, more efficiently. That's the ascension of your tactical growth.

Tactical

The tactical requirement actually has two parts. The first is being able to recognize what is happening on the field. The second is being able to make a decision that will help your team the most and hurt the other team the most. So your tactical requirements are having the awareness as to what is going on in the game by seeing it, then having the decision-making process to sort out what's best. And what is best is going to be determined by a lot of different factors - what third of the field you are on, your match-up, time and space, and whether you have possession etc.

This article is reprinted with permission from The Sport Source, 2000 Soccer, Official Athletic College Guide.

Anson Dorrance is the highly successful coach of the University of North Carolina women's program. His best selling book <u>Training Soccer Champions</u> is available by calling (800)331-5191.

WHAT DOES IT TAKE TO PLAY IN COLLEGE

BY G. GUERRIERI

The question "what it takes for a player to compete as a college soccer student-athlete" is constantly brought before me in my travels across the nation. The answer may be as broad and vague as the question.

In this book (The Sport Source, 2000 Soccer, Official Athletic Guide) you will find hundreds of soccer programs. Is there a soccer program for you? Yes. Can you walk into any program and compete immediately? No.

To compete as an NCAA Division I player, a student-athlete must be focused, dedicated and opportunistic. However, to play college soccer you don't have to do it at the Division I level.

NCAA Division I is the most recognized level of college soccer. Players and coaches put in long hours to insure success and development. These hours (12-20 per week, depending on the team) are in addition to college classes, individual study and social activities. The time commitment of a Division I player is likened to a full-time job which thousands of players line up for every year.

Speed is the primary component that distinguishes a Division I player from Division II, Division III and NAIA. The technical speed of a player to take control of the ball and do it with as few touches as possible separates the top Division I player from all others. The tactical speed to read and anticipate two or three passes ahead of play rather than just reacting to the current pass, run or clearance determines the speed of the game, and thus the level of play from Division I (tactically fastest) down. The physical speed of a player is the most obvious. If players are always getting away from you, maybe you should look for a lower level of play where you can compete with success.

College coaches receive letters and phone calls every week from high school players, coaches and parents claiming that they have a player that can play Division I soccer. The college coach's first questions are always "Have you ever seen my team play?" and "Do you know what the Division I level is like?" Too often they don't. They have only seen youth and high school games and are not aware of the speed of play at the college level. The same could be said of college coaches pushing their players to the pro or international level; we don't always get a chance truly to see that game, and naturally think that our most talented players can excel at that level without truly understanding what that level demands.

A quality Division I player typically has a clear repertoire of attributes to bring to a college team. Here are examples of the capabilities of a typical Division I player:

Forwards:
- Possess the physical speed necessary to break away from strong tenacious markers.
- Able to hold and shield the ball with the head up while teammates move into support roles.
- Show confidence and talent to take on 1, 2, 3 players en route to goal.
- Comfortable and successful with both feet while under pressure.
- Have superior physical fitness.

Midfielders:
- Have superior physical fitness.
- Are physically strong and quick to avoid injury through collision and physical play.
- Possess the tactical ability to read and play within the tempo of the game.
- Show the technical ability to play a controlled one- and two-touch game.
- Able to play the ball from side to side as well as back to front of the team.
- Can and will defend anytime the ball is lost.
- Have the personality to play under pressure.

Defenders:
- Possess the physical speed and strength to keep up with the nation's top strikers.
- Have the grit and determination to play within a team's defensive system.
- Show the technical ability to play accurate 40-yard passes to teammates and to control long pass from opponents.
- Display the ability to win 50/50 challenges consistently.
- Have the composure to play and create (not just destroy).

Goalkeepers:
- Have the stature and physique that bring confidence to their teammates.
- Have the strength and ability to win 50/50 balls and avoid injury.
- Display the technical ability to make 100% of the saves in the middle two-thirds of goal and many of the bigger saves in the corners.
- Possess the leadership and social skills to get along with players and lead defense.
- Ability to distribute the ball safely in their own half of the field and penetrate the other team's half with long punts, throws or drop kicks.
- Willingness to work as hard in training as in games.
- Display the tactical ability to play within the flow of the game.

This article is reprinted with permission from The Sport Source, 2000 Soccer, Official Athletic College Guide.

Coach G Guerrieri has been the Head Women's Soccer Coach at Texas A&M since 1993. G also worked several years as a SoccerPlus Goalkeeper School Director.

FINDING THE RIGHT COLLEGE

You are a serious soccer player with proven skills. It only makes sense to begin your college search with the top NCAA Division I programs, right? Maybe not. Despite your interest in soccer, a college education is the pathway to a career that lasts a lifetime. Remember: opportunities in professional soccer are rare. Even for those who do play professionally, the average retirement age for soccer players is the late 20s. So how do you find the right school to meet both your immediate soccer interests and your long-term career goals? There are two primary steps.

First, do your homework. Think about your education first. Research the colleges and universities that offer programs in your areas of interest. For example, if you want to study engineering, compare the schools with the strongest engineering programs, and list the strong and weak points of each. Remember, however, that many students change majors at least once in their college careers, so don't lock yourself into a school with too many limitations.

Compare the types of programs. What are your main interests? If they are many and varied, look for schools with comprehensive selections of programs and a traditional curriculum of studies from architecture to zoology.

Are you interested in a faculty dedicated to teaching undergraduate studies? A university with a large graduate population may have professors whose classroom syllabus reflects the most current research, but have limited availability for extra-hour undergraduate assistance.

Do you desire innovative programs with independent study, cooperative work/study, or overseas study programs? Or do you want a more structured, traditional program built around core requirements which must be completed prior to specialized study in a specific major?

Other things to consider are the size and geographical location of the school. What type of environment are you used to in your high school? Is it a large school in an urban or heavily populated suburban area? You might feel isolated at a small school or in a small community. Do you enjoy small classes where the students and teachers know each other well? Large universities may have lecture classes of several hundred students where you are simply a name on a test booklet or term paper and will be required to use self-discipline to attend classes and keep up with the assignments. Large schools will have more social opportunities and extra-curricular activities; small schools will offer fewer, but more intimate, social networks and smaller classes.

Are you a Southerner who longs for snow? Maybe you're a Midwesterner eager to experience the West. Consider your background and experience and how they may differ from another region of the country. The cultures and lifestyles vary as much as the weather as you move from region to region.

Once you have made a list of schools which offer the size, region, types of programs, and educational opportunities you desire, it's time to take the second step.

Do a first-rate job of presenting yourself to the school.

The application is your first and most important presentation of yourself to the school. The application must be typed, with no spots, stains, corrections, or errors. It should be well-organized and signed and contain correct grammar and spelling. Complete it and return it early. Make it look and read professional.

Next, initiate a personal interview. This requires neat and appropriate dress. Don't neglect your hair, face and fingernails. Be overdressed rather than underdressed. Make your appointment well in advance and arrive on time or slightly early. If you are unavoidably detained, call and let the person know you will be late.

Visits initiated by the athletic department and possible interviews with an alumnus are other opportunities for you to present yourself to the school. In each case, the aim is always the same: you want to create the most positive impression you can without being dishonest. Don't try to fake it. Be genuine and spontaneous, but be well-prepared.

Your list of schools should be appropriate to your long-term goals. Narrow the list down as you research, and contact each school and athletic department. Think of your application as a professional job resume.

Know as much as you can about each school before you visit. Don't risk embarrassing yourself by asking about a program the school doesn't offer.

As your list comes together you will discover the right school for you. Your hard work has enabled you to prove yourself on the pitch. Now put the same effort into preparing yourself for a lifetime.

Reprinted with permission of Student Athlete Magazine (see page 143)

We must either find a way or make one.

Hannibal

HOW TO WRITE COVER LETTERS TO COLLEGE COACHES

"You now have 45 seconds of my undivided attention"

College soccer coaches get hundreds of letters every year from high school seniors who want to play in college. Unfortunately, this can become mind-boggling for the coach. In most cases, the coach hands this part of recruiting over to his assistant coach.

Usually, the assistant coach is overworked too, so your letter may only get **a few seconds of attention**. It is important that you clearly show the things that the coach wants to see in your cover letter and your resume.

Too many resumes are cluttered with unnecessary information. We recently saw a resume mentioning that a player could type 60 wpm, and have seen numerous resumes with information that is **totally useless to the college coach**. If a college coach is going to look at your information for only 30-45 seconds, then the things that **they** are interest in had better jump off the pages.

This is where you can use your typing skills. Select large, legible fonts. Sign the cover letter, but avoid handwriting elsewhere.

Here are some tips:

1. Don't start your letter off with a line like "Dear Coach" and make it a form letter that you send to a list of schools that you are interested in. Take the time to find out the coach's name so that it starts out, at least, "Dear Coach Nelson,"

2. Make sure your letter explains why you want to go to his school. Is it because the school has a great computer science program that interests you? Is it because you like the location of the campus? College coaches still get these generic letters that say, "Dear Coach, I want to play soccer in college. Could you send me information about your school and soccer scholarships for your team? Sincerely, Joe Bagadonuts"

3. Make sure that you place your name, address and phone number on every page of your cover letter and resume! Coaches have offices crowded with papers, books, equipment and "stuff." If your envelope gets buried in "the stack" he might not be able to find your address or phone number. So he has to wait for you to call him. We know of several coaches who get over 300 letters a year from high school seniors. It's very easy to get lost in the shuffle.

4. If you are going to be in any big tournaments or a tournament that you think

he might be at, tell him. Specify your club name, jersey color and number; this information is very important. If he can't watch, he may send someone, or know someone in the area who could watch your game. They use their net works this way.

5. Sum up your resume in the letter. You don't have to say, "I feel that I can play for you because..." but say something like, "The last two years I have been on my state's ODP team," or "my team recently won these two tournaments," or something that interests the coach so that he gives your resume more than a quick glance before he puts it "in the stack."

6. Your resume should have your academic information on it. List your grade point average. If your school uses something other that the standard 4.0 scale, explain it. List ACT or SAT scores, as well as class rank (class rank is calculated by the end of your Junior year at most schools). Coaches are looking for two things here. Are you able to handle his school's academics and, if so, are your grades strong enough to earn merit scholarship money.

7. If you are good in other sports, especially track or cross-country, include them. If you set the school record in the 200 meter run, say so, and include your time.

8. Include soccer experience that carries a lot of weight. For example, success at the Olympic Development level, generally, means more to a college coach than the fact that your team won the high school state championship. Also, include your success with the club team. The problem with high school soccer, generally speaking, is that the quality of players throughout the league isn't always that strong. Scoring 100 goals in 2 high school seasons doesn't carry as much weight as making the ODP state team.
Include your success at the high school level but put ODP or club success first. If you didn't do so well at ODP try-out at least mention that you were a participant.

9. You don't have to list all of the soccer that you ever played. Keep it brief so he will read it all. Just include your high school information, club information and honors, like ODP teams or high school all-league or All-State. Coaches still get resumes that say the person was a member of the photography club!

10. References on your resume should be ODP coaches, college coaches, or top club coaches. The college coach may not know your high school coach. List the best coaches in the area you can find. Ask them if you can use them as a reference, and tell them why, so they will be prepared when a coach calls.

Some sample cover letters

Your letters should be a little longer; these examples are just to get you started.

Dear Coach Kelly,

I will be graduating this spring, and I am considering attending State University. I have heard a lot of great things about the school's International Business program. I would like to enroll in that program.

I would also like to play soccer at your school. I have made the State team in the Olympic Development Program for the last two years. I have also started on my high school team all four years.

Could you please send me some information on your soccer program and the possibilities of a scholarship

Dear Coach O'Brien,

I am graduating from high school this spring and would like to play soccer in college. Although I don't know a lot about your school, I have heard great things about your soccer team. I recently saw your team play against State two weeks ago. I also saw an article in a magazine about your program.

I have been a starter on my high school and my club team for the last three years. Both have been League champs. I have attended SoccerPlus Camps for the last three years.

I would like to study English, and Education. Please send information regarding your school and the soccer program. Enclosed please find my soccer resume.

Reprinted with permission of Student Athlete Magazine (see page 143)

Courage is resistance to fear, mastery of fear – not absence of fear.
Mark Twain

HOW TO PLAN AND CONDUCT A CAMPUS VISIT

When to Go

The best time to visit your future college is the fall of your senior year. Cliff McCrath, head coach at Seattle Pacific University, and one of the most successful college coaches in the country, suggests you visit and apply to the schools in the fall so you can watch the teams play. And there are also financial aid reasons.

"Most financial aid is a combination of 'need' and 'scholarship' money. Need-based funds are announced in April. Seniors may be unable to receive aid if they start looking in spring." With schools able to sign players in February, most of the 'scholarship' money, for new and returning players, is gone by March.

Unfortunately, many people like to visit colleges in the summer, trying to tie the visit in with the family's vacation.

McCrath says, "To visit the school in the summer to see the physical campus is fine. But, in terms of getting an idea of the personality of the campus, students, etc. The campus is usually barren at this time of year. Be sure and look at the school again in the Fall."

What to Look at on Campus

You have to turn into a detective. Remember, you are going to spend at least four years at the school.

Coach McCrath suggests you investigate the following: The dorms - find out everything that you can about them. The Student Union Building - notice the type of people that hang around the building. Are these people friendly? Are they relaxed, polite? If you can have a car, is there a safe place to park it? How far would it be from where you live? McCrath admits that this may sound trivial now, but it is amazing how a little thing can turn into a major problem. Consider the security and the location of the school. We met a student who visited a very small school and remarked how beautiful the school and scenery was. After three months there, she absolutely hated the fact that everything was an hour's walk away and freshmen couldn't have cars.

Where are most of your classes going to be? Are new buildings being built, or has everything been the same for the past half century? How far is it to the nearest mall, theater? What hours are the stores open? Where is the bank? The laundry?

Find out everything you can. The good and the bad. Then decide if you can live with the bad. Don't just listen to the campus tour people, walk around on your own and look at things. Pick up the school's newspaper and the city's newspaper and see what people are talking about on the editorial page. What issues face the campus? How will they affect you?

What to Look at on the Field

On your campus visit, one of the most important things you can do is watch your future team play. This can give you ideas about the kind of success you may have at the school. Try to sit on the bench during the game. Be in the locker room before the game, during half time, and after the game.

Watch their style of play. Are they playing balls into space? Do they play the ball to feet? Are they extremely defense minded? Are they a physical team? Is this the way you play, or would like to play? Can you contribute?

While the team is playing, watch the coach. Is he constantly directing the game or screaming at players? Can you handle that? Is the coach just sitting there like a statue showing no emotion of any kind? What is he like before the game? What is he like during half time? What is he like when someone makes a mistake or the team gets scored on? What is he like when his team scores? What is he like under pressure?

Can you handle four years of this kind of environment? Be honest!

Questions to Ask

We know of a player who was transferring from one college to another. He knew that the next school would probably be his last. It showed in the questions he asked. He had many more than the usual high school Senior, because he knew what questions to ask.

Don't be afraid to ask too many questions. Also, ask different people the same question. Especially if someone says something bad, get a second opinion. Don't speak only with the soccer people. Talk to anyone. Don't be shy. It's your future!

- What are the training sessions like?
- What is study hall like and how many times a week do you attend?
- What is curfew like?
- What is preseason like?
- Where do you stay on road trips?
- What about missed classes because of soccer games?
- What do you eat on road trips?
- What do you have to buy for road trips and during the season?
- How many other recruits have you had on campus? What positions did they play? Where are they from?
- Has anyone transferred from the team recently? Why?
- What other schools were you looking at?
- Why did you choose this school?
- If you couldn't play soccer anymore would you still stay here?
- How much soccer do you play in the off season? Is it required?
- How many students per class? What do you do in your spare time?

Questions They May Ask You

While you are asking questions about the school, the soccer team, and the coach, people will be asking you some questions. Here are some questions you may be asked and some suggestions.

Have you applied to the school yet, and/or filled out financial aid forms?

Most coaches won't talk to you until you have been accepted. Most coaches won't talk scholarship money until you have filled out financial aid forms.

What other schools are you looking at? Tell the coach the truth. This gives him an idea of where he stands. If his is the only non-nationally-ranked school on your list, it may give him an idea. The coach also knows what the other schools have in scholarship money and what types of players those schools are looking for. Also, it gives him an idea of how you fit in academically. It never hurts to say where you're looking. It helps you both.

What are your strengths and weaknesses? This is no time to be modest and it is no time to lie. Think about and prepare your answers. You are selling yourself. Don't waste this chance by saying you're not sure. Tell him the truth and be specific. If you're the fastest thing in the State of Ohio, tell him!

Where does our school rank on your list? This tells him how much of a chance he has with you. If his school is number five on your list he knows it will take a lot of work to sign you. If you say number three, and he knows the other two schools can't offer you much money, or his academic programs are better, he knows what to tell you. Whatever you do, don't lie.

Last Spring, a college coach we know was recruiting two players extremely hard. He thought he had them for sure. They kept telling him "yes" on the phone, but, none of their paper work was in. Finally, they told him that they decided to go to another school. This hurt him. He had told other players that he didn't have money for them. He was saving it for these two recruits. If these two had said "no" early, the coach could have signed two players who wanted to go to his school and needed the money. Even if there is no scholarship money involved don't string the coach along.

How big of a scholarship are you looking for? When college coaches are reviewing our publications, this is one question they hate to see. When we meet with players and parents, this question always comes up. The best overall strategy is to defer answering with any specific amount until you have completed all your college visits. Gradually, you will be able to put a "price" on playing for each school...and those prices will often be quite different!

Reprinted with permission of Student Athlete Magazine (see page 143)

PAYING FOR COLLEGE

When to Start

In the college selection process there is one area that everyone...coaches, players and parents feel uneasy about...the Financial Aid Form (FAF). To try and get scholarship money through the financial aid form, involves a lot of research, a lot of paperwork, and a lot of communication among the parents, the player and the coach of your future college. The person who has to begin this ground work is the player. Your Senior year is the wrong time to start. It is best to start looking in your Junior year, and this means spending hours in the library reading books during your free time.

To prepare most of our brochures we contact college coaches. In this case, we didn't. We started talking to them and they kept saying "I don't know." We went straight to the Financial Aid officers and Directors of several colleges and universities all over the United States. After dozens of phone calls and letters and conversations we have published some of the most important tips that they can offer.

The Student Athlete Magazine contains a regular section entitled "Money For College" in which scholarships of particular interest to student athletes are discussed. In addition, scholarships which are funded by The Instep and/or its advertisers specifically for soccer players are described.

The magazine also frequently contains articles relating to "The Financial Package", i.e., the sum of scholarships (athletic and merit), grants, work-study and loans which are offered to the student athlete by the college.

The Form

The first mistake high school Seniors make is that they pick up the FAF near the first of the year. Don't. The forms are usually available at your school by the first of November.

These forms should be at your high school, if they are not, then call another high school. If that is no help, then call a local college. You don't have to be considering that college to get a form from them. You can't send them in until the first of the year, so don't worry about filling it out right away, just have it finished by January first. The financial aid packages are announced in April so, if you don't have it in by the deadline, it will be too late to even be considered. All money is distributed on a first come first serve basis. You may hear people complain that they have kids in school already, and don't make enough money and they didn't get any financial aid in the past. Ask them when they sent their FAF, you will often hear a date well past the first week in January. First come first serve.

Deadline II

To make things a little more confusing, colleges have their own deadlines as well. So, let's say you were a little lazy, and you sent in your form on Feb. 1st. You specified that it be sent to State University. Well, State University may have a deadline until which they will accept forms. If their deadline is January 31st, they won't consider you. The best way to avoid trouble is to submit your form during the first week of January. Each school has a different deadline, so you have to check with them. Once again, you avoid all of this if you send it in by the first week in January.

Form II

If you haven't already become frustrated with this whole process, you are doing well, but there is one more thing you should know. Every person in this country who wants to go to school fills out the US Government FAF form. Unfortunately, some schools have their own financial aid form as well. These schools will not consider you unless you have filled out their form in addition to the FAF. They are not trying to be mean, but some schools get thousands and thousands of these FAF forms per year. The mere task of telling every student that they have to fill out another form must be extremely tedious. Someone is bound to be missed. Or if you do get a notice about it, it could easily be put in your "stack" somewhere.

The best thing to do, would be to call and ask. Of course they won't tell you to do this because they don't want thousands of calls. But they do install an automated telephone answering system which, when it is not continuously busy, can provide information. In addition, carefully read the application documentation to determine if they have a separate financial form for you to fill out.

If an additional form is required, check the deadline for submission, and do whatever you have to do to obtain a form and turn it in on time. A strategy for beating the crowd is to call the financial aid office at every school you are considering in September, when they can easily be reached by phone. Ask your questions. Have their packages sent to you for use at your convenience.

Financial Aid Myth #1

Say you take our advice and you get the FAF on December 1st. You rush home with it to your parents and say, "We need to get this in the mail on January 2nd." The first thing your parents will see are the earnings questions, and they may say that you have to wait until they get their W-2 from their employers.

This is the number one reason why people don't submit it in time.

On the form you will notice that there is a place to declare how much you made and another for estimating your salary. Estimate your salary by using your year-to-date-information found on your pay stub. Later, schools may ask to see a record of the actual income and taxes you filed. In short, don't allow the excuse that you have to wait for your W-2's from your employer. It could cost you your financial aid.

Financial Aid Myth #2

The next most frequent problem that delays the form is the question, "What schools do you want the form sent to?" In November or December, high school Seniors are not sure where they want to go. They wait, until they have a better idea of which schools they are considering before submitting the form. This is a major mistake! List the schools you are thinking about attending. Mail the FAF in as soon as you can. Of course, be sure to call those schools to see if they have a separate form as well. If you decide on another school you would like to consider, don't worry. There is another form that allows you to append additional schools to your list.

Other Sources of Money

You need to check other sources of money as well. One source most would never expect is your State Government. For example, if you graduated from a Florida high school with a 3.0 GPA and you attend college in Florida, you get money from the State Government. A grant is credited against your balance. Each state is different, and the programs vary, but don't discount a school because of it's cost. Use different programs to get some money from each. It can add up! If you live in the state of Pennsylvania, Vermont, or Rhode Island you get compensation for attending a private college in any state, providing that you qualify. Once again, the only way you can qualify is to get your form in early. There could be restrictions, so you need to check it out with your high school counselor, or the financial aid departments at colleges you may attend. There are thousands of private scholarships from corporations, colleges, clubs, and individuals. There are a number of massive books in the reference section of your library called scholarship directories. They are categorized in many different ways: geography, interest, parents' background, careers, religion, etc. In addition, there are computerized scholarship search services that charge a fee to do research for you. If you look carefully, you should find a few that you can apply for. Because research requires so much reading and so much correspondence, it is best to start on this during your Junior year. Another reason is that many of these scholarships have timetables, or ask for information that could take months to compile.

Other Things You Should Know

This problem is rare, but it does happen. Let's say you choose a school that costs $10,000 per year. You fill out your financial aid form and are eligible to receive $2,000. Your soccer scholarship from the school is for $8,000. You think, "Great, the whole thing is paid for." The US government can have something to say.

On the financial aid form, the government specifies what they think you can afford to pay. In this example, they feel that you can afford to pay $2,000. Uncle Sam tells your school, "Either we are going to take away the $2,000 or you are." The school always takes away the $2,000. Now, instead of getting $10,000, you receive $8,000. Six from the school and two from the government. This rarely happens. If it does, you must recognize that it is legitimate, and based on your reported ability to pay. On the bright side, it usually only happens at inexpensive colleges, which are virtually nonexistent today.

Work-Study. Work-study is a job that you can qualify for, based on your FAF. The job is part-time and on campus. Most allow you to study while doing your job. For example, working at an information desk, answering phones, etc. Schools have different policies. By law they must give you a pay check. But they can require you to sign it over to the school to pay for the balance of your education. Or, you may be allowed to cash it and use it as you wish. Every school's policy is different.

Reprinted with permission of Student Athlete Magazine (see page 143)

You do not merely want to be considered just the best of the best. You want to be considered the only ones who do what you do.

Jerry Garcia – The Grateful Dead

You learn you can do your best even when it is hard, even when you're tired and maybe hurting a little bit. It feels good to show some courage.

Joe Namath

SUGGESTED READING FOR COLLEGE

College Eligibility Requirements for the Student Athlete
The following is a list of invaluable resources for anyone who is considering playing soccer in college.

NCAA Rules: **NCAA guide for the College-Bound Student Athlete**
To get a copy write to
> NCAA
> 6201 College Blvd.
> Overland Park, KS 66211
> Phone (913) 339-1906
> www.ncaa.org

NAIA Rules: **NAIA guide for College Bound Student Athletes**
To get a copy write to:
> NAIA Headquarters
> 6120 South Yale, Suite 1450
> Tulsa, OK 74136
> Phone (918) 494-8828
> www.naia.org

Recommended Reading

The Sports Source: Official Soccer College Guide 2000
Over 1,000 page book dedicated to giving student athletes information about every college soccer program in the US. Information includes cost of colleges, degrees, scholarships available, Soccer coaches names, addresses and phone numbers. And much, much more. To order call (800)331-5191. Cost $19.95

Student Athlete Magazine
Student Athlete magazine is published quarterly by the Student Athlete Scholarship Foundation. It is loaded with tips and advice for high school soccer players and their parents. The magazine takes you step by step from your freshman year making sure you know all the do's and don'ts. Cost $20 for 4 issues
For more information:
(800) 506-7257
www.student-Athlete.net

EXTRA DIMENSION

CONSISTENCY
BY G. GUERRIERI

A quality goalkeeper can strengthen every team. But what's the most important quality in a "quality" keeper?

Countless variables contribute to success: size, coordination, agility, quickness, courage, leadership ability, shot-stopping technique, tactical awareness, etc. Across the nation, goalkeepers are trained on different aspects of the position; however, in many cases the keeper is merely "taken through the paces" physically, rather than being taught responsibilities, or shown how to prevent goals. What, then, should the average coach stress to his or her keeper? The answer is one word: consistency.

The greatest gift a keeper can give is consistent stability to the defense. There is almost nothing more frustrating than to have your team play well, offensively and defensively, for an entire match - and then give up a silly goal, due to the keeper. Nothing takes the competitive edge out of your team more.

I have the luxury of working with some very good goalkeepers. The paramount message I try to teach is a simple one: "Don't give up soft goals! "We use simple physiology to teach our keepers to work within their physical limits - rather than working against their bodies. We push ourselves in training to learn our limits; then concentrate on playing within those limits during games. For example, every year goals are scored because the goalkeeper took off for a crossed ball that he or she had no business going after - thus leaving the goal unattended, and the ball bouncing around in shooting range. The catch phrase we use in this instance is "only go after balls you can get - and get every ball you go after." Otherwise, the keeper should stay in goal, and depend on shot-stopping abilities.

Very few keepers win championships single-handedly. However, multitudes of keepers cost their teams games - and probable championships. We've all seen the keeper who makes the amazing, fully extended diving save in the upper corner, then five minutes later lets a slow roller beat him near post.

Many of the game's greatest goalkeepers are in their late 30s, even early 40s. How did they stay successful? They always make the simple save, and use their experience to anticipate what type of shot may be coming, so they make mostly simple saves. Yes, they can make the extraordinary diving save - but the simple ones are their meat and potatoes. The rest is merely gravy.

Train your goalkeeper to always be able to make the easy save - every single time. Train your keeper to be the leader of your defense; to help him or her anticipate play, and position himself or herself to consistently make easier saves, rather than depend on acrobatic ones. Train your keeper to understand that everyone gives up a goal at one time or other, and that all that can be done is learn why it was scored, to prevent repeats of the same one. Train your keeper to understand that if he or she is scored upon, the opponent must earn it. I always hear that goal-keepers are different kind of creatures - flakes, who just aren't playing with a full deck. The more you as a coach believe this, and allow the keeper to operate outside the limits of your other players, the more you send the message that you don't expect him or her to operate within the team. Demand consistent behavior, make sure he or she understands the objectives of the team, and that you only expect him or her to make ordinary saves - and I think you'll find that the more comfortable the keeper becomes within those limits, the more he or she will actually begin adding stability to your team.

❝

No matter how good you are there's a lot of luck involved.

Reggie Miller

I'm a great believer in luck and I find the harder I work, the more I have of it.

Thomas Jefferson

GOALKEEPER'S PREGAME WARM-UP

Before the whistle blows to start the game the goalkeeper must feel confident that he has done a good job preparing his mind and body to play in the game. This preparation usually begins long before the game. The last 30 minutes are the most critical but there are some key issues that also must be dealt with the day of the game.

The first of these is to make sure your equipment is in order. Your cleats should be polished and your gloves should be clean. Take time when you are packing your bag that you have all the equipment you might need; an extra pair of gloves, extra shoe laces, water bottle, small towel etc. as well as all the other obvious equipment. The second consideration is what you eat the day of the game. Obviously it depends on what time of day your game is but there are some definite do's and don'ts. Do eat foods that are high in carbohydrates like pasta, bread, fruit and vegetables. Don't eat hot dogs, burgers, doughnuts or potato chips. These foods are high in fat and take a long time to digest.

The third consideration is always giving yourself extra time to get to the game. If you have to rush to get to the game you will likely become anxious. By leaving early you protect yourself from any unforeseen delays and allow yourself to focus on the game while en route to the field.

THE WARM UP

1. Before you do anything with the ball take a little jog and some skipping to increase your body temperature. As you start to warm up stretch all the major body parts. Once you feel that you have broken a sweat start playing the ball with your feet back and forth with a teammate. Mix up your passes in the air and on the ground. Passes should be 15 to 30 yards long.

2. Have your training partner strike balls towards you from about 12 yards away. These balls should be played within your control zone i.e. you should not have to dive to save the ball. You partner should supply you with a variety of shots to handle.

3. Lie down on your right hand side with the ball in your hands as if you had just made a save. Roll the ball to your partner who is 10 yards away. Get up to make a save to your left side. Repeat until you make 10 to 15 saves on each side.

4. Start off 15 yards away from your partner. Roll the ball to his feet. As your partner dribbles the ball toward you, come out and make an appropriate breakaway save. Please note that your training partner should avoid physical contact with you. Make 5 saves on each side.

5. Step into the goal. Partner lines up shots from the edge of the 18-yard box. Each shot is taken from a different angle and distance. Varity of shots should include chips, volleys, low driven balls and balls placed into the

corners. Make 15-20 saves.

6. Set up the balls at the upper corner of the 18-yard box. Partner sends over a variety of crosses from different angles. If you have plenty of balls goal keepers should distribute the ball to the opposite side with an overarm throw. If you only have a few balls (1-5) you should throw the ball back out to the server after making a save. Alternate sides after 15-20 saves.

7. You should work a little on foot distribution by taking some goal kicks, drop kicks and punts. You should also strike 5-10 back passes that are played along the ground into their box. These balls should be hit first time.

By now you have covered most scenarios that you will encounter in the game. Some teams like to do shooting exercises before the game starts. If your team does this share the responsibility with the back up goalkeeper. Make sure the exercise is realistic and that you have a chance to make saves. Remember that your responsibility is to get yourself ready to play. If you are getting bombarded with shots get out.

Take some time to collect your thoughts and focus on what your goals are for the game. Refill your water bottle. Talk to your teammates, especially your defenders, about areas of concern that the team may have addressed in practice during the week.

This whole routine should take approximately 30 minutes. However, you should do this routine at practice to see how long it takes you and then you can make adjustments if necessary.

There will be times, especially at tournaments when you will not have the luxury of 30 minutes to warm up on the field. In those cases you must do as much as possible off the field. Don't get flustered. When you get onto the field maximize your time in the goal.

Every goalkeeper will have his or her own routine for warm up. The one outlined above is used by youth, collegiate and professional goalkeepers. It will certainly prepare you to play but it may not totally suit you. What's important is that you do have a set routine and you cover the 7 key elements of the warm up. When the whistle blows are you ready to play?

7 Key Elements of the Pregame Warm-up:
1. Increase body temperature and stretch before any diving or kicking.
2. Basic handling before diving.
3. Progression of diving saves.
4. Shot handling
5. Breakaways with no contact
6. Crosses from both sides
7. Distribution (hand and foot)

"

It's what you learn after you know it all that counts.

John Wooden, UCLA Basketball

Setting a goal is not the main thing. It is deciding how you will go about achieving it and staying with that plan.

Tom Landry, Dallas Cowboys

"

THE BACK-UP GOALKEEPER

If you coach a team with only one goalkeeper then your troubles with backups and playing time will only effect the players on your bench. However, many coaches are dealt with the situation of having two goalkeepers. One goalkeeper may be the clear "starter" but how will you manage keeping the backup part of the team?

If you are stuck in this situation you have to make a very important decision that will greatly affect the happiness of your goalkeepers and perhaps your team's chemistry as well. Here are some options with advantages and disadvantages to think about when making your decision:

OPTION 1

- Play your starting goalkeeper for the majority of the game until the result of the game becomes apparent (For example your team is winning 5-0).

> **Advantages:** Your starting goalkeeper gets all the starts, and is in the game during crucial moments.
>
> **Disadvantages**: Your back-up goalkeeper never knows when he will get a chance to play, and when he does get into the game it is just "garbage time". You have a lot of your subs in the game and the quality of play is not very high. Because a lot of subs are in the game your back-up goalkeeper will have no interaction with the rest of the starting line-up. There will be no cohesion with communication or the speed of play if your backup never has the opportunity to play with the starters. It will also be very tough to keep your backup goalkeeper training with enthusiasm during the season if he never knows when he will be playing.

OPTION 2

- Play the starting goalkeeper for the first half of each game and your backup goalkeeper for the second half of the game.

> **Advantages**: Your goalkeepers get equal amount of playing time, so if your starting goalkeeper gets hurt right before the post-season then you have yourself a second goalkeeper who has played just as much as your starter.
>
> **Disadvantages:** Your defense will have to adjust to a different goalkeeper with different characteristics and habits during halftime, and because of this a mistake can occur in the early going of the second half. The situation will also arise where you have to send in the backup keeper for the second half of a 0-0 game. So when the other team scores with five minutes to play and your team ends up losing two games in a row by a score of 1-0, where do you think the team is going to place the

blame? This is a situation where the team loses all its confidence in the backup goalkeeper. Another tough situation for the backup goalkeeper is if he is called to start the second half of a game that your team is losing 3-0. Who wants to come into the game in that circumstance? Do you want your backup goalkeeper playing all the second halves of games if your team consistently plays better in the first half and slacks off in the second half?

OPTION 3

- Play the better goalkeeper for the entire game against all of the tough competition and important games and allow your backup to play a couple of games against the teams you know will be an easy match.

> **Advantages**: Your starting Goalkeeper gets quality starts and the back up still gets some playing time. The backup also can prepare for games he knows he will be playing in.
>
> **Disadvantages:** If your starting goalkeeper gets injured, then your backup is thrown into the starting role without a lot of quality playing time. This situation could also affect your team's chemistry. How will your players react when they know your backup keeper is starting the next game, or what if your backup keeper is not as popular with the rest of the team as your starting goalkeeper? Whoever is in the net greatly affects the level of play of the teammates in front of him. This will also restrict the amount of time your team has to experiment with different styles of play. For example if your team wants to try playing zone defense against a weaker team, then your starting goalkeeper won't be exposed to the system of play and has to watch from the bench.

OPTION 4

- Alternate games, the first goalkeeper plays a full game and then the backup goalkeeper plays the next full game.

> **Advantages:** Most goalkeepers would prefer to alternate games rather than split halves. This gives the goalkeeper the opportunity to play his/her own game. The goalkeepers also know when and where they will be playing and have the opportunity to prepare during training for the upcoming opponent.
>
> **Disadvantages:** If one goalkeeper is playing poorly for a couple of games, then the next time that goalkeeper is scheduled to play your team might not respond well because of lost confidence in that goalkeeper. It is tough for your goalkeepers to train at a consistent level during practice when they know they will only be playing every other game. You won't be able to play to the strength and weaknesses of your opponent. For example you are playing against a team who likes to play "long ball" that will create a lot of breakaway situations, your starting

goalkeeper can handle breakaways with ease but today is your backup goalkeeper's turn to start. This could also reflect badly on the coach, as some people will view your decision to alternate games as indecision and maybe even a lack of knowledge of the goalkeeper position.

Whatever situation you choose you have to be confident that your goalkeepers and the players in front of them are comfortable with the set up. You may decide to go with one of these options or a combination of several options to create your own solution to the backup dilemma. Let us know your thoughts and how you handle this situation.

HOW TO SURVIVE A HIGH SCHOOL SEASON WITHOUT A GOALKEEPER COACH

Not every school is fortunate enough to have a goalkeeper coach. Those coaches who are afforded the luxury often consider themselves quite lucky. Goalkeepers at all levels have frequently expressed their preference to be trained by qualified goalkeeper coaches. But in the real world we know that teams with goalkeeper coaches are the exception rather than the rule. Obviously that leaves the majority of coaches pondering the question "How will I survive the season without a goalkeeper coach?"

The reality of the situation is that if no one else can coach the goalkeepers then the job is yours. You have probably found yourself wearing many different hats as a coach; Nurse, weight trainer, conditioning consultant, guidance counselor, bus driver, fund raiser, laundry specialist, psychologist etc. etc. etc. As coach you are responsible for the well being of your team and you are constantly filling in gaps as needed. If the gear is dirty and you are the only one to wash it then you need to learn how to do laundry (assuming you have never done laundry before). Your goal is to get the gear clean. You do not necessarily want to become the best laundry person in the country and you probably have no desire in learning what all 15 settings on the machine do. You don't particularly care about all the different types of fabric. You only want to know enough to get the job done. Coaching goalkeepers is not much different. But just like doing laundry you need to know some things before you get started.

The essentials of goalkeeper coaching are learning the basic techniques and using the correct terminology. The basic techniques are stance, catching and diving. If you know nothing else about goalkeeping you should be familiar with those three techniques. The correct terminology is important for credibility with your keeper. You may not be able to walk the walk but you have to be able to talk the talk. Goalkeepers can be compared to animals. They can sense fear. If you are uncomfortable or afraid of the topic their respect for you will diminish. On the contrary, if you are comfortable discussing goalkeeping they will embrace you. Goalkeeper education is available in many places. There are numerous goalkeeping videos on the market. Avoid the action packed tapes and seek out those produced by top class goalkeeper coaches such as "Goalkeeping-The DiCicco Method" by former US national Team Coach Tony DiCicco. In the off-season make a point of attending goalkeeping clinics. If you have the time attend a week of Goalkeeper School for coaches or enroll in an NSCAA Goalkeeping Diploma Course. (Many high school coaches require their goalkeepers to attend a week of summer camp at

Goalkeeper School.) If a local College or University in your area has a goalkeeper coach ask if you can sit in and observe a session.

Once the season comes along, the work you did in the off-season will pay dividends. As your team starts training devote every fifth session to your goalkeeper. You can do this in two ways. First, plan your session so that the goalkeeper will get plenty of action. The subject can range from shot stopping to crosses to back passes. It does not matter as long as your goalkeepers are heavily involved. Second, position yourself directly behind the goalkeepers and coach them throughout the session. For this session they are your focus of attention. Resist the temptation to get caught up in what the field players are doing. They will most likely have your attention for the next four training sessions.

Many goalkeepers in the past have said that they feel insulted when the coach tells them to go over to a corner of the field and "do your goalkeeper stuff" until I call you back over. Unsupervised the goalkeepers achieve very little. Goalkeepers do need time together training but it must be structured. Never ask your goalkeepers to do something that you have not done with them previously. Before you send them to one side tell them specifically what you would like them to do. As a leader on the team the goalkeeper should be aware of your demands for a high level of work ethic while being relatively unsupervised. This is a great time for footwork training or any technical training with multiple repetitions.

As important as it is for goalkeepers to train alone it is just as important for them to train with the team, even when they are not the focus of attention. The benefits to this include better team chemistry, improved awareness of the goalkeeper of team tactics and opportunities for goalkeepers to work on their field playing skills.

Once a week it is a good idea for the coach to train the goalkeepers for 30-45 minutes on their own. This can be done easily before practice. Trust your captains to organize the team warm-up while you train the goalkeepers. At this time you can identify specific issues or areas of concern with the goalkeepers. Most of this training will be technical and the goalkeepers can repeat the exercises performed at a later session when they work on their own. Without doubt these sessions will improve your relationship with your goalkeepers and help to develop you into the goalkeeper coach that you thought you never had.

FUN AND COMPETITIVE GAMES FOR GOALKEEPERS

Every coach and goalkeeper is faced with the problem of how to make his or her practice sessions interesting and stimulating. Nobody wants to go through the same routine at practice every time. We need new exercises and goals to help us maximize our effort when we train.

Let's face it. Most training sessions are based around the field players on the team. As a result goalkeepers must be creative in using the time allotted to them to train exclusively on goalkeeping. Since goalkeepers often train without a coach it can help if the practices are as competitive as possible to ensure a high level of intensity.

Here are a couple of games that you can try at practice. Many goalkeepers have thoroughly enjoyed playing different versions of keeper wars at camp but since most players do not have access to portable goals I have only included games that require one full size goal.

Rooster game
Keepers start on the ground sitting down with their legs out in front of them. Coach bounces ball in front of them. Both goalkeepers get to their feet and challenge for the ball.

Gloves game
Place a glove on the ground and each goalkeeper steps back 5 yards. Upon the coach's command the goalkeepers approach the glove. The object is to pick up the glove and get back to your starting point without being tagged. You can only be tagged when holding the glove.

Crossbar game
Keepers take turns trying to hit the crossbar with hand or foot service from 18 yards. As an extra challenge start the goalkeeper in a push up position. Each goalkeeper gets 10 attempts. Whoever hits the crossbar most wins.

One on One Goalkeeper Challenge (All services with the hand).
Full size goals and two small goals made with cones 2 yards apart.

Goalkeeper gets 10 chances to beat opponent from 18 yards. If the keeper saves and holds the ball he can shoot on mini goals placed on either side of the shooter. The shooter then must try and prevent a goal being scored in the mini goals. Shooter keeps shooting until goalkeeper holds a save.

One on One Goalkeeper Challenge (All services with the feet).
Attack mini goals.
Same as above but now shots are taken with feet.

Shootout at 10 paces
Goalkeepers square off 10 yards apart, each standing in a 6-yard goal with a ball in hand in a position ready to throw. Upon the coach's command goalkeepers throw the ball in hand and attempt to save the ball being thrown at them. (Tip: make sure you have extra balls ready)

House of pain
1v1 plus a coach in a 10 x 10 yard grid. Coach plays with whoever has possession. Keeper with the ball can only use feet. Defending goalkeeper attempts to win the ball back in breakaway fashion. Upon winning the ball the goalkeeper becomes a field player and plays with the coach.

Dunking Balls
Goalkeeper needs to dunk 6 balls over the crossbar while doing a push up in between dunks. Dunks must be made with two hands. If goalkeeper is unable to dunk he should jump as high as possible and throw the ball over using both hands. The competition is against the clock.

The object of these games is to increase the competitive spirit at practice while allowing your keepers to have fun.

You have no control over what the other guy does. You only have control over what you do.

A J Kitt, Race car driver

Winning isn't everything. Wanting to is!

Anon.

GOALKEEPER EQUIPMENT

GLOVE SELECTION

Goalkeeper gloves are one of - if not the most - important pieces of equipment you can possess. However, most goalkeepers choose gloves that have nothing to do with the requirements or needs of that particular keeper.

Climate, surface, durability and budget are a few criteria you should use when selecting a goalkeeper glove.

The best wet weather glove is an all white, super-soft latex foam palm. This offers the best coefficient of friction to the synthetic ball surfaces used today. The down side of the foam surface is that it is the least durable.

If you play in dry conditions most of the year, this glove may not be necessary. In that case a textured palm, such as injected or stipple foam, or some form of sublimation on the palm, will offer greater durability (with a small sacrifice on gripping).

Most gloves do not offer serious warmth or dryness, although some very expensive models now feature Goretex construction. Be careful to pick out the necessary function from the gimmicks (in other words, how warm do your goalkeeper gloves really need to be?).

The best strategy is to have a practice model (inexpensive gloves, or your previous game gloves). Do not use your match gloves in training! Keep them just for games. Your old game gloves can get pretty ugly and raunchy, but they can hang in there as practice gloves for longer than you think (Just don't bring them inside the house).

Plan on going through more than one game glove in a season, so make sure you don't spend your whole budget on that first pair. Keep your gloves as clean as possible, by hand-washing them with lukewarm water. Make sure you allow them to dry naturally - not in sunlight or near a heater.

Some gloves actually work better slightly wet or damp (especially the latex foam models). Others work equally well wet or dry, while some definitely work better dry.

Know what you are buying! Goalkeeper gloves are indeed highly technical equipment that will help you be a better keeper - but remember, the hands are the key element in catching. The gloves only assist!

Getting the right fit for your gloves is just as important as the style you have selected.

When you are looking for a goalkeeper glove for indoor you look for a glove that is durable yet gives you the grip that you are used to outside. When you are looking for a training glove you look for an inexpensive glove that you can abuse during practice.

There aren't as many options however, for the fit of your gloves. The performance of your equipment depends heavily on the fit.

The basic rule of thumb is to fit your gloves with some extra space at the end of the finger-tips. Most people would say about 1/2 inch is enough. If your gloves fit too snug then your fingers will have no room to move when your hands need to conform to the shape of the ball during catching or even worse, forget about trying to box the ball. If your gloves are too big then your hands will get lost inside all that foam and just as having shoes too big, you will lose all your touch on the ball. Also, take into consideration the wrist enclosure for your gloves, is it too bulky or will it come undone easily?

GLOVE CARE

Goalkeeper gloves are high performance equipment. Extensive care is needed to prolong the life and save the quality of your gloves. The more dirt your gloves collect, the less effective they become. There are a lot of myths about the proper way to clean your gloves such as putting them in the washer, wearing them in the shower, etc. After years of "trial and error" and dozens of suggestions, the best way to clean your gloves is this easy five-step method.

1. Rinse gloves thoroughly in the sink using warm water.
2. Squeeze out the excess dirt and place the gloves in the sink with the palms facing up. With the water still running, rub your thumb along the foam palm pushing the dirt out of the glove. You should start to see the original color of the foam returning as you push the dirt out.
3. Using the same motion as in Step 2, now work shampoo into the glove. Continue to use the shampoo until the original color of the palm completely returns. Note: for some reason inexpensive shampoo seems to work best.
4. Rinse glove of any remaining dirt and suds. Now is also a good time to clean the Velcro wrist enclosure. Pick out any lint or dirt that will prevent the Velcro from holding itself closed during use.
5. Allow the gloves to sit at room temperature and away from direct light until they are as dry as you want them (if you like to play with your gloves slightly damp do not let them dry completely). Finally, put your gloves in a "glove bag". Most companies who make keeper gloves also make glove bags to keep your gloves in good condition.

Goalkeeper gloves are expensive, and could cost you anywhere up to $125. Unfortunately, no company gives you a guarantee on the deterioration of the gloves they make; so try to use your old gloves for practice and new gloves for games.

SHOE SELECTION

Goalkeepers have different gloves for different conditions (i.e. wet, dry, indoor), it is also a good idea to have several different types of footwear for the many conditions a goalkeeper may face.

Think about it, you're in your club team's championship game for the spring season and all of a sudden at the end of the first half it starts to rain. To this point you have had your regular hard ground molded shoes on. As the horn signaling the end of the half sounds the score is even at 0-0. You walk back onto the field for the second half still wearing your molded shoes, mad at yourself for not buying that pair of screw-ins in the local soccer shop that you have been eyeing for the past few weeks. Things go well for you in the first few minutes of the second half, but as your defense breaks down late in the game, you face a breakaway that threatens your shutout. As you come out to cut down the angle, you slip and the striker calmly dribbles the ball around as you lay there in the mud. The striker slips the ball into the back of the net and is mobbed by his teammates. It was the only goal you gave up that game, but you know you would have been in a better position to make the save if you had those screw-ins.

Although you don't need screw-ins all the time, it is extremely comforting to know that they are sitting in your bag under the bench if you need them. If you are able to afford it, there are four types of shoes that you might need during the year: Indoor=Flats, soft-ground = screw-ins, hard-ground = regular molded, and extremely hard ground = turf or multi-stud.

There are many things to consider during your selection of a new pair of shoes. Here are some questions to ask yourself before that big purchase:

How much money do I have to work with?

The newest pair of shoes at the store might cost up to $150. Remember, the most expensive shoes might not be the best for you. These new shoes with new manufacturer gimmicks will tend to go down in price after the current season.

How can I tell what shoes fit the best?

Be familiar with what type of feet you have (wide, narrow, long, etc). Different manufacturer's shoes tend to "run" differently. Adidas shoes are usually narrow, Puma shoes are normally wider than most and Nike or Kelme are known to run true to size. To ensure a good fit be sure to try on both shoes, some people have one foot that is larger than the other. After you have laced up the shoes compare the rows of eyelets. If the rows of eyelets are not parallel up the length of the shoe then the shoe is not your size. For example: if the eyelets at the bottom of your shoe are closer than the eyelets at the top than the shoe is too narrow. Or if the eyelets at the top are wider than the eyelets at the bottom or if the rows are too close together up the length of the shoe then the shoe is too wide. Now take a walk around the room to see if the shoes hurt your feet anywhere.

Soccer shoes are performance equipment and they should not have the same fit as your every-day shoes. Soccer players (goalkeepers too) must use their feet, so the trick is to get your toes as close to the edge of the shoe as possible as long as it is comfortable on your foot. Remember that the higher quality of leather that you buy, the more the shoe will stretch and mold to your feet. Don't buy a shoe that is too big because your parents say that you're growing fast and it will last for a couple of seasons. If your shoes are too big you risk injury to yourself, your shoes will fall apart more quickly and you will be sacrificing your touch on the ball.

Do I have any problems with my feet?

If you tend to get blisters or aching heels after you play, then you probably have the wrong kind of shoes for your feet. A lot of these problems can be solved by getting the right fit, however there are a couple of other things to consider when getting your next pair of shoes. To reduce the impact of running around for 90 minutes on hard ground you might want to purchase a shoe with a multi stud design. The idea is the more cleats on the bottom of the shoe the better your weight will be distributed during each stride. There are also shoes on the market with soft soles and cleats that will absorb the shock better than a hard stud will.

Remember that comfort is the most important thing to consider when buying your shoes. Try to get your shoes from a soccer specialty store. They will have a knowledgeable salesperson who can help you with the many options available. Try to buy your shoes well before your season starts, this will allow you to break them in before your first game. When you are using your new shoes have your old shoes under the bench. If you feel a blister coming on you can change into your old shoes for the rest of your training.

SHOE CARE

Just like your gloves, you need to keep your shoes clean and well managed to increase performance. Avoid walking on concrete or taking your shoes off without untying them. It is important to take care of your shoes if you want them to last. And when you walk onto the field, your appearance is a direct reflection of yourself. If your shoes are polished and ready, then you are probably ready as well.

To keep your shoes in top shape make the following a habit:

1. Remove all dirt from your shoes with a damp cloth after each use.
2. Apply leather conditioner with a cloth while the shoes are still moist. Water allows the leather pores to open, and the conditioner to penetrate.
3. Stuff your shoes with newspaper between use, especially if they are wet.
4. Allow your shoe to dry away from direct heat or sunlight.
5. Polish your shoes with a wax polish occasionally for a high gloss.

YOU ARE THE REF

1. If the ball from an indirect free-kick touches another player and enters the goal should a goal be awarded?

Yes, however, in the case of a free kick taken by a defender in his own penalty-area the kick must be retaken.

2. May a free-kick be taken by lifting the ball with both feet simultaneously?

No. It is not accepted that a free-kick is taken correctly if it is lifted with both feet.

3. If the referee forgets to raise his arm when an indirect free-kick is taken, does this mean that this indirect free-kick has not been carried out in accordance with the laws?

No. The award of an indirect free-kick shall be respected, because the initial offense requiring an indirect free-kick is not nullified by the referee's mistake.

4. If the cross-bar becomes displaced through breakage or faulty construction in a match played under the rules of a competition and there are no available means of repairing or replacing it, should the match be abandoned?

Yes. The crossbar may not be substituted by a rope in order to finish the match.

5. If a goalkeeper draws unauthorized marks on the field of play with his foot, what action should the referee take?

If the referee notices this being done during the match, he need not interrupt the game just to caution the player who is making unauthorized marks on the field of play after the match has been started. The player concerned must be cautioned for ungentlemanly conduct when there is an interruption in the game. If however the referee notices this before the match starts, then he shall caution the offending player immediately.

6. What action should the referee take if a defending player moves beyond his goal-line in order to place an opponent in an off-sides position?

The action of the defender is considered as ungentlemanly conduct, but it is not necessary for the referee to stop play immediately to caution the player. The attacker should not be punished for the position in which he has been unfairly placed.

7. A spectator blows a whistle and the goalkeeper, thinking that it was the referee, passes the ball to a teammate who picks up the ball and places it on the ground, assuming that a free kick has been awarded. Should the referee award a free kick

or penalty for handling the ball or should he stop the game because of the spectator's intervention and resume play by dropping the ball?

Because the whistle came from off the field and not from the referee, a direct kick (or PK) shall be awarded to the opposing team for handling the ball.

8. The ball accidentally hits the referee or a linesman on the field of play and rebounds into goal. What should the referee decision be?

The referee shall award the goal.

9. If an opponent stands in front of a player at a throw-in to impede him, what action should the referee take?

Allow the throw-in to be taken if the opponent remains stationary. But if he moves or gesticulates to distract the thrower, he shall be cautioned for ungentlemanly conduct.

10. May the advantage clause be applied if a throw-in taken incorrectly sends the ball directly to an opponent?

No. The throw-in shall be retaken by a player of the opposing team.

11. After Team A has kicked the ball into the goal of Team B, the referee notices a signal from his linesman. The linesman tells the ref that a few seconds before the ball entered the goal of Team B, the goalkeeper of Team A had punched an opponent within his own penalty-area. What action should the referee take?

The goal shall not be awarded, the GK of Team A should be sent off and a PK shall be awarded to Team B.

12. Should the referee award a PK if a player other than the GK takes a goal-kick and the ball passes out of the Penalty area into play but is blown back by a strong wind without any other player having touched it, and a player of the defending side other than the GK plays the ball with his hand within the penalty area?

Yes. If in similar circumstances, the GK takes the Goal-kick and tries to stop the ball entering the goal and just touches the ball with his hand but fails to prevent it passing into the goal, the referee shall award an indirect free kick.

13. During a goal-kick, the ball has traveled the distance of its circumference without leaving the penalty area when an opponent enters the penalty area and is intentionally fouled by a defending player. Can a PK be awarded?

No, because the ball was not in play at the time the offense was committed. The offending player shall be cautioned or sent off, according to the nature of the offense, and the goal kick retaken. If the ball has passed outside the penalty area before the game is stopped, a goal kick shall still be retaken as the player of the attacking side entered the penalty-area before the ball was in play.

14. If, due to a collision with an opponent, a player loses a shoe and immediately scores a goal, is the goal valid or not?

The goal is valid. The player did not intentionally play barefoot, but lost his shoe by accident.

15. If the color of the shirts of the two goalkeepers is the same, what should the referee do if neither has another shirt to change into?

The referee shall allow play to continue.

16. If a penalty kick is retaken because the GK moved his feet, must the same player take the kick again or could another player to do so?

Another player could also retake the PK.

17) Is a player taking a PK allowed to place the ball elsewhere than on the penalty mark owing to the water-logged state of the pitch?

No.

18. What action should the referee take against players who leave the field of play while celebrating a goal?

Celebrating a goal is part of soccer. A caution is only warranted if a player gives an excessive demonstration of jubilation, e.g. by jumping over the boundary fence, gesticulating at his opponents or the spectators or ridiculing them by pointing to his shirt.

19. Should the referee send off, for violent conduct, a player who spits at an opponent?

Yes. Play shall be restarted with a direct free kick (or PK) if the offense took place while the ball was in play.

Besides pride, loyalty, discipline, heart and mind, confidence is the key to all locks.

Joe Paterno, Penn State Football

Only those who dare to fail greatly can ever achieve greatly.

Robert Kennedy, Attorney General

DICICCO METHOD VIDEO SERIES

This comprehensive 3-tape series provides a detailed and organized presentation for keepers and coaches. Each video is loaded with progressional drills and training tips that will improve any goalkeeper's or coach's understanding of the position. With demonstrations from both male and female goalkeepers at the high school, collegiate, and international levels, this series is designed for all levels of keepers and coaches.

Tape #1 Introduction of Goalkeeping
"What Every Goalkeeper and Coach Needs to Know"

Tape #2 Goalkeeper Training and Coaching
"The Techniques and Tactics of Modern Goalkeeping"

Tape #3 The Goalkeeper as a Team Player
"The Tactical, Psychological and Physical Dimensions"

$29.95 Each or $79.95 for all three • To order call 800-331-5191.

REEDSWAIN BOOKS

**#788 Zone Play: A
Tactical and
Technical Handbook**
Pereni and Di Cesare
$14.95

**#794 248 Drills for
Attacking Soccer**
$14.95
by Allessandro Del Freo

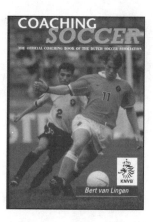

#154 Coaching Soccer
$14.95
by Bert van Lingen

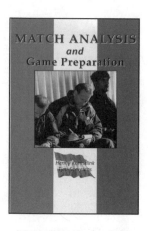

**#261 Match Analysis
and Game
Preparation**
$12.95
*by Kormelink and
Seeverens*

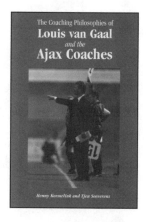

**#177 Principles of
Brazilian Soccer**
*by Jose' Thadeu
Goncalves*
$16.95

**#175 The Coaching
Philosophies of Louis
van Gaal and the
Ajax Coaches**
*by Kormelink and
Seeverens*
$14.95

REEDSWAIN • 1-800-331-5191 • www.reedswain.com

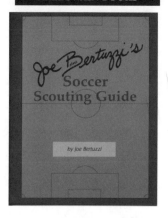

**#785 Complete Book
of Soccer Restart
Plays**
*by Mario Bonfanti and
Angelo Pereni*
$14.95

**#789 Soccer Scouting
Guide**
by Joe Bertuzzi
$12.95

**#284 The Dutch
Coaching Notebook**
$14.95

**#765 Attacking
Schemes and Training
Exercises**
by Fascetti and Scaia
$14.95

**#185 Conditioning for
Soccer**
Dr. Raymond Verheijen
$19.95

#786 Soccer Nutrition
by Enrico Arcelli
$10.95

REEDSWAIN • 1-800-331-5191 • www.reedswain.com

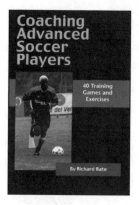

#244 Coaching the 4-4-2
by Marziali and Mora
$14.95

#291 Soccer Fitness Training *by Enrico Arcelli and Ferretto Ferretti*
$12.95

#169 Coaching Advanced Soccer Players
by Richard Bate
$12.95

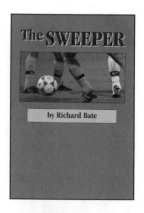

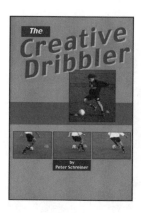

#225 The Sweeper
by Richard Bate
$9.95

#792 120 Competitive Games and Exercises for Soccer
by Nicola Pica
$14.95

#256 The Creative Dribbler
by Peter Schreiner
$14.95

REEDSWAIN • 1-800-331-5191 • www.reedswain.com